JED JOHNSON

JED JOHNSON: OPULENT RESTRAINT

INTERIORS

EDITED BY TEMO CALLAHAN AND TOM CASHIN

RIZZOLI
NEW YORK

First published in the United States of America in 2005

by Rizzoli International Publications, Inc.

300 Park Avenue South, New York, New York 10010

www.rizzoliusa.com

Editors: Temo Callahan, Tom Cashin

Art Direction & Design: Takaaki Matsumoto, Matsumoto Incorporated

2005 2006 2007 2008 / 10 9 8 7 6 5 4 3 2 1

Printed in China

ISBN: 0-8478-2714-3

Library of Congress Catalog Control Number: 2005928871

Frontispiece: Portrait of Jed Johnson by Francesco Scavullo, 1972

LAUNCHING A CAREER

BY PIERRE BERGÉ

I met Jed Johnson when I was introduced to Andy Warhol, and I immediately took a liking to this timid, handsome, blond-haired boy. At the time I had no idea of his talent as an interior designer. It was only later, when I decided to acquire an apartment in New York, that I discovered him. It was he who suggested that I should opt for an "American" space—in other words, one filled with American furniture, American objects, and American paintings. How could I ever forget that visit to Mark Twain's house when I discovered, with wonder, the beauty of the stencils? It was then that I decided to entrust Jed with the apartment.

I had already bought a few paintings myself, but with Jed I found all of my eighteenth- and nineteenth-century furniture, made by renowned cabinetmakers in Philadelphia and Chicago. Together we bought the Tiffany lamps and tables, and when everything was complete, I had the feeling that I was living in a magical place.

It was Jed's first commission, and I am proud to have given it to him. From that day on, the affection I felt for him was doubled by admiration. An interior designer was born, and in some ways, I had contributed to the process. He went on to build a successful career, and we can be sure that he would have continued to astound had death not taken him from us.

That day, I knew that I had lost a very dear friend, a true artist present at important moments in my life. That day, I knew that I would never forget him.

The elaborate stenciling and superb American furniture and objects in the New York apartment of Pierre Bergé caused a sensation and launched the decorating career of Jed Johnson.

Photograph: John Hall

ON JED JOHNSON

BY PAUL GOLDBERGER

In an age noted for its "signature" designs, Jed Johnson's signature was grace. Johnson became one of the most celebrated interior designers of our time not by inventing a style or by creating anything anyone might call a "look." I suspect he would have hated the very notion of an easily identifiable trademark to his work. He seemed to have had a love of all styles and sought only to practice them softly and respectfully. He was so earnest in his belief that design should rise above gimmicks that you would think he would have been bound to fail in a time that is as susceptible to the lure of simple tricks as ours is, not to mention as suspicious of the sincerity that goes hand in hand with earnestness. Jed Johnson was as far from cynical as a designer could be. He believed in the power of objects—no designer could not—but he never fell prey to the cult of the perfect object or to the belief that beautiful things are all that is needed to make life worthwhile.

Johnson managed to work with an extraordinary roster of celebrity clients without losing what may be the rarest quality of all in design work today, which is unselfconsciousness. No one could call Jed Johnson hesitant; if there was anything that marked his designs, it was a forthright determination to make space resonate, to make it glow with that peculiar form of perfection that comes when objects of great quality are well-placed in carefully wrought surroundings. He did not care whether the objects were Art Deco French sofas or Arts & Crafts tables; the point was that they had to be good, and they had to fit together in a room, which was mainly a matter of some hard-to-fathom formula that existed in his intuition. Another way to say all of this is to say that Jed Johnson had an eye, one of the best eyes that has existed in our time.

He could be a wonderful innovator. He took great delight in finding new materials, new textures, and new combinations of things that would assure that his work was fresh, not

In 1991 Johnson and his partner, architect Alan Wanzenberg, were asked by the magazine *Metropolitan Home* to design a room in a charity showhouse, benefiting the design industry's effort to combat AIDS. The room featured walls of green-tinted plaster on a copper mesh. The effect was extraordinary and a perfect background for classic, mid-twentieth-century furnishings by Pierre Chareau, Gerrit Rietveld, and Eugène Printz.

Photograph: Lizzie Himmel

archaeological. He and his partner, the architect Alan Wanzenberg, almost single-handedly brought back Pewabic and Fulper, glazed tiles that had mostly been out of production until Johnson and Wanzenberg became intrigued by them more than two decades ago. In 1991 their room of khaki green–pigmented plaster troweled over copper mesh, designed as part of a showhouse to benefit the Design Industries Foundation Fighting AIDS, was the talk of the exhibition. And could anyone other than Jed Johnson put together furniture by Émile-Jacques Ruhlmann and Jean-Michel Frank, walls of satinwood and hand-woven silk, and paintings by Picasso, Léger, Klee, and Miró and make the whole thing seem not pretentious but relaxed and gracious? That particular combination occurred in a stunning Fifth Avenue apartment that is one of Johnson's masterworks, but its easy, natural air is not unique. It is also present in the ornate classical moldings on oceanic themes or the bathroom lined entirely in shells designed for the sumptuous Shingle Style house of Barbaralee Diamonstein and Carl Spielvogel in Southampton, Long Island, gestures that from another designer might have seemed contrived, but in Johnson's hand they come off as completely unforced.

Like a great film director who knows how to marshal vast resources to create flawlessly composed, intimate scenes, Jed Johnson designed rooms that were elaborately wrought but had the gift of feeling simple. This is particularly so in the West Side apartment he and Wanzenberg shared, in an old studio building with a double-height living room. Johnson's love of texture and soft, muted color and his deep fondness for Arts & Crafts design, which did not ebb even as he discovered other styles, all flowered here first. And as the apartment evolved, that period continued to set the theme. Arts & Crafts fit his sensibility perfectly: strong, direct, clear, yet full of subtlety, intricacy, and texture; here it feels both down to earth and sublime. Johnson, along with Wanzenberg, not only collected furniture by Gustav Stickley and objects by Charles Voysey, Louis J. Millet, and others, but he also knew when to stop. He could mix Stickley with Warhol, and nothing disturbed him more than a room designed as a museum-like period piece. If his eye had too much discipline to permit him to mix and match with the wild abandon of the true eclectic, it was also too imaginative to let him be content with the static quality of a room that was frozen at an arbitrary moment in history. And so he took pleasure in careful, precise juxtapositions, using design as a way of pointing out the kinship between Art Deco and the French furniture that preceded it, for example. He loved objects, but he never worshiped them. That alone distinguished him from many of his colleagues, some of whom have never quite understood the difference between connoisseurship and emotional attachment. Jed Johnson did not look to things for spiritual satisfaction, but they nonetheless aroused his passions, and he knew furniture and fabrics as well as any scholar. "He might forget someone's name, but he would remember a piece of furniture he had seen ten years earlier," Wanzenberg said not long after Johnson's death.

There was a spareness to Johnson's designs that reflected his personality: no wasted words, no unnecessary objects. A Jed Johnson room had just the right amount of air and space, just as there were always pleasant but never awkward silences in his slow, precise conversations. He was no minimalist, given his love of sensual textures and rich materials, but nothing he did could be described as overstuffed, either. Excess to him was a form of vulgarity. He was a natural editor and

The beauty of the hand-cut and glazed tiles from the Pewabic and Fulper tileworks fascinated Johnson. He used them frequently in projects and helped bring many of the companies' discontinued designs back from oblivion. The luxurious Pewabic-tiled bathroom in the Manhattan apartment of Caroline and Michel Zaleski was completed in 1994.

Photograph: Elizabeth Heyert

had enough self-confidence to edit himself best of all. Although his aesthetic was not in any way literally Japanese, he seemed instinctively to embrace the essential quality of Japanese design, which achieves the greatest richness in the process of paring down to elegant essentials.

In the years before his death, his practice grew so substantial that it seems, at first, curious that his career began in Andy Warhol's Factory. He started as a young assistant who had dropped out of school and worked his way up to the status of underground filmmaker. As he moved into Warhol's inner circle, his extraordinary eye joined with Warhol's obsessive acquisitiveness to direct and shape the artist's collecting. Warhol would cast the net wide, buying vast lots of antiques, furniture, collectible objects, and art, and Johnson would edit it, sifting through the trove to select the best pieces and then placing them. Soon Johnson was directing not Warhol's films but his life; he found the artist his townhouse on East Sixty-sixth Street, designed its interiors, and lived there with him for a time.

It was not a great leap from Johnson's partnership with Warhol to Sandra and Peter Brant, the collectors and patrons who had helped finance Warhol's magazine, *Interview*. They took great delight in Johnson's sensibility and ultimately commissioned him, and later him and Wanzenberg, to design eleven different projects, ranging from the interiors of their Greenwich, Connecticut, mansion designed by Allan Greenberg to a Robert Venturi–designed house in Vail, Colorado. By the time of the Vail house, client and designer had grown so close that they decided to own the house together, and they built it jointly. Later Johnson did most of his work with Wanzenberg, but he took pleasure in collaborating with other architects as well and designed interiors for houses by Cesar Pelli, Hugh Newell Jacobsen, Samuel White, and others. The Brants were the bridge between the world of Warhol and the world of independent clients, and they commissioned some of Johnson and Wanzenberg's most important work, such as the restoration of several historic buildings on Conyers Farm, the huge estate in Greenwich that they developed into an exclusive luxury community.

Johnson's Warhol connections helped bring in numerous celebrity clients, such as Mick Jagger and Jerry Hall, Barbra Streisand, and Richard Gere. But the fame of his client list gives a misleading impression of his career as a whole. Much of his finest work was done for people whose names were not household words, people who came to him because they were as serious as he was about design and connoisseurship. He took great joy, too, in helping friends live in surroundings better than what they might have achieved on their own. The writer Fran Lebowitz, who knew him from the Warhol days, could not afford to live like a typical Jed Johnson client, but he continually sent her furniture anyway. "It pained Jed to see people he liked not have the best," she explains. "The extraordinary thing is how Jed, who was so interested in artifice, was so completely free of it himself." As Sandra Brant says, "He was always clear about what mattered, always down to earth and yet always able to recognize someone or something that had magic. Jed was that person people don't think exists anymore: He was pure, gentle, and modest. But look at his work, and the beauty and magic come through, quietly."

The shell-encrusted powder room Johnson designed for the Southampton house of Barbaralee Diamonstein and Carl Spielvogel is ornately classical yet whimsical and natural.

WORKING WITH JED

BY ARTHUR DUNNAM

Working with Jed Johnson was an incredible learning experience. I had longed to find a design firm that would expect more from me and give me an opportunity to grow. In 1987, when I joined Jed's firm, I found exactly what I had been looking for. I discovered a new level of approaching a project: with an informed historical perspective, consideration of the architecture and location, and intense scrutiny of the lifestyle of the client. Jed, who had no formal schooling in design, would commence each new commission by spending hours scouring his extensive library for appropriate visual references. In his years with Andy Warhol, Jed saw some of the truly amazing residences of the day. His careful eye for detail and an equally impressive memory assured that bits of all he saw found their way into his design work. His hours of research for each job were augmented by endless miles of travel for his shopping expeditions. As my years of shopping with Jed progressed, and I accompanied him on his rounds to the finest antique dealers in London and Paris, I gained an appreciation for his embrace of the entire spectrum of art and objects, not falling into the trap of limiting one's interests to only the most elevated. He certainly had an eye for the very best, but Jed could also appreciate the fun and interesting as well.

Jed had a particular affinity for textiles, especially antique or made in the spirit of the original, using period looms, correct fiber content, and subtle, custom colorations. He often explored and utilized suppliers of whom most American designers had never heard. The wondrous silks, linens, and wools that appointed a Jed Johnson interior came from tiny mills throughout the world specializing in "couture" fabrics for the interior. He loved the deliciously quirky patterns as well as obscure period designs that he often specially colored to create environments that whispered luxury and were so enviably perfect that they appeared undecorated, as if they had magically always existed.

The Manhattan apartment of Maureen and Marshall Cogan, even with the finest mid-twentieth-century furnishings and art, is comfortable and relaxed. A crystal and silver lamp by Émile-Jacques Ruhlmann rests beneath a Picasso drawing in the couple's master bedroom. The chair is by André Groult.

Jed's work was always a studied amalgam of exquisite period furnishings and meticulously designed contemporary elements that complemented and completed the environment. Jed traveled endlessly to find the perfect antiques; for newly created furnishings, he would spend hours finding image references and more hours refining shop drawings, until every detail adhered to his perfect sense of proportion. An essential ingredient in this equation was the host of artisans who would carve, sculpt, forge, gild, paint, or otherwise conjure the ideas that Jed devised. They all loved to be involved in creating a Jed Johnson interior, not only because the design was so wonderful but also because they knew how much Jed respected their abilities and truly appreciated their efforts and the end result.

In addition to his discerning eye for interior decoration, Jed also had a broad knowledge of and an infallible sensibility for interior architecture. He worked frequently with his partner Alan Wanzenberg. Alan's years of formal education were a wonderful complement to Jed's perspective and his love of period detail. While they both shared a passion for contemporary and twentieth-century architecture, as well as English and American Arts & Crafts, Jed also appreciated great English and French architecture of the seventeenth, eighteenth, and nineteenth centuries. Most evenings in the office would find Jed stopping at a drawing board or two for one last look to make certain that the details he envisioned appeared on the paper just so.

Period reference formed the basis of his work, but Jed also strove to infuse his work with a clean, modern edge. His style followed the Babe Paley directive to remove one accessory from an outfit before leaving the house. It's that little bit of restraint that keeps a person and a room from appearing overly put together. Jed would design custom trimmings that, although luxurious, were the same color as the rest of the piece; the multiple tones of wall-panel glazing might be so subtly differentiated that they appeared to be shadows. These measures and many others assured that Jed's rooms only slowly revealed themselves to a visitor. Like Jed himself, his interiors were quiet, but when one spent time with them, the remarkable details and quality emerged. They proved to be the kind of timeless spaces that never go out of style because they were never based in trends of the moment.

Were Jed with us today, I am certain that his work would still be at the forefront of design, valued for its ability to reflect what is current while evoking the best of the past. I also know that he would be immensely pleased that the firm that bears his name continues to uphold the standards, practices, and overall design direction that he established.

In collaboration with design associate Arthur Dunnam, Johnson created a nineteenth-century Orientalist fantasy for the Chieftains charity showhouse in Greenwich, Connecticut, 1987.

Photograph: John Hall

ANDY WARHOL

NEW YORK CITY

1977

It can be argued that Jed Johnson became an interior designer purely in self-defense. In 1968 he moved in with Pop artist Andy Warhol and had to deal with the vast collection of everything acquired by the legendary, compulsive shopper or be buried by it. His editing skills and natural eye were sharpened by the arduous experience.

When, in 1974, Warhol and he moved to a Federal-style, red-brick, East Side townhouse, it automatically became Johnson's design school and decorating laboratory. In the 1987 Sotheby's auction catalogue of the Warhol estate, Johnson wrote, "I oversaw the move from his small house on Lexington Avenue to the six-story townhouse on East Sixty-sixth. . . . He encouraged me to shop for appropriate furniture to fill up those spaces. By this time he'd visited enough rich people's houses to know what they looked like when they were done well."

Johnson visited many "rich people's houses" himself and many beautiful and historic homes. One of his favorites was the Mark Twain house in Hartford, Connecticut, splendidly decorated with late nineteenth-century hand stenciling. It was love at first sight. He was determined to revive the technique long in disuse in American décor. With painstaking period research and the best craftsmen, his results were spectacular. Warhol loved to visit his beautiful rooms, but his obsession with privacy permitted few guests. He lived in the bedroom with his television, telephone, and dachshunds.

The various rooms differed by period and style as Johnson learned and experimented; some Federal, some Victorian, one Art Deco, all interesting and beautiful and filled with the best American antiques. With a natural sense of scale, proportion and color, he made few mistakes. His years of self-education made him an expert in decorative arts history and a true connoisseur, yet he always remained humble and self-deprecating about his lack of formal training.

The Warhol townhouse was a triumph of restrained richness and style and laid the foundation for what Warhol glibly called Johnson's "fancy decorating company."

Preceding page: Jed Johnson's fondness for stenciling grew from his visits to great nineteenth-century American houses. An American mid-nineteenth-century Rococo chandelier hangs from the hand-stenciled Orientalist medallion on the ceiling of the bedroom he occupied in Andy Warhol's Manhattan townhouse between 1974 and 1980.

Opposite: The mid-nineteenth-century white marble fireplace in Johnson's fourth-floor bedroom is a perfect foil for the colorful stencil design of stylized tulips. The mosaic tile hearth, faux-grained woodwork, and period motif carpet completed the extraordinary picture.

Photographs, pages 19–29: Norman McGrath

Left: Andy Warhol's Federal parlor contained an array of fine American furniture from the first half of the nineteenth century. To complement it, Johnson chose a lustrous, medium-toned, yellow-green color for the walls and designed period-style window treatments with handmade silk trimmings to contrast. Gilt-bronze medallions embrace the symmetrical curtain panels. Between the windows a fine, Philadelphia carved and inlaid secretary, circa 1820, stands as though waiting for the placid lady with a pink bonnet from the nineteenth-century English portrait to sit and finish her letter. A matching pair of 1835 Philadelphia mahogany recamiers flank the fireplace, facing each other across a painted and stenciled center table attributed to the nineteenth-century Baltimore furniture maker John Finlay. The armchairs seem comfortable and inviting despite their classical formality. As though hiding, an early twentieth-century Egyptian Revival parcel gilt and painted chair can be spied beyond the fireplace. The carpet is Aubusson circa 1900. Many visitors were surprised that none of Warhol's own art hung anywhere in the house.

Overleaf: Johnson utilized early nineteenth-century French, hand-blocked wallpaper panels (probably Zuber) beneath the dado in Warhol's bedroom. A white marble, Grecian-style dancing figure ornaments the fireplace, looking as though, at any moment, she might step down.

Preceding page: In Johnson's bedroom a late nineteenth-century bronze Mercury is pursued by a flying heron. A Franz Hagenauer sculpture views the scene discreetly from behind a silk lampas curtain.

Right: In the Art Deco sitting room, Johnson kept the palette cool and modern. Roy Lichtenstein's *Laughing Cat* greets the eye initially, then the rest of the art and the furniture comes into focus. An Émile-Jacques Ruhlmann cabinet rests between the windows. The pair of lacquered chairs and the "eggshell"-topped low table are by the French master Jean Dunand. The Pierre Legrain mirrored shagreen cabinet supports the 1915 bronze *Head of Venus* by Pierre-Auguste Renoir; behind it, *Feminine Painting* by Man Ray. A Cy Twombly rests on an easel in front of the mantel, which holds a 1952 polished-bronze sculpture by Jean Arp.

A Federal mahogany bed dominates Andy Warhol's bedroom. The carved and painted tester is draped in a period manner; according to Johnson, "The canopy was a favorite hiding place for Andy's jewelry." The painting is attributed to the early nineteenth-century American artist John S. Blunt. The bedside lamp is Tiffany, circa 1910.

PIERRE BERGÉ

NEW YORK CITY

1978

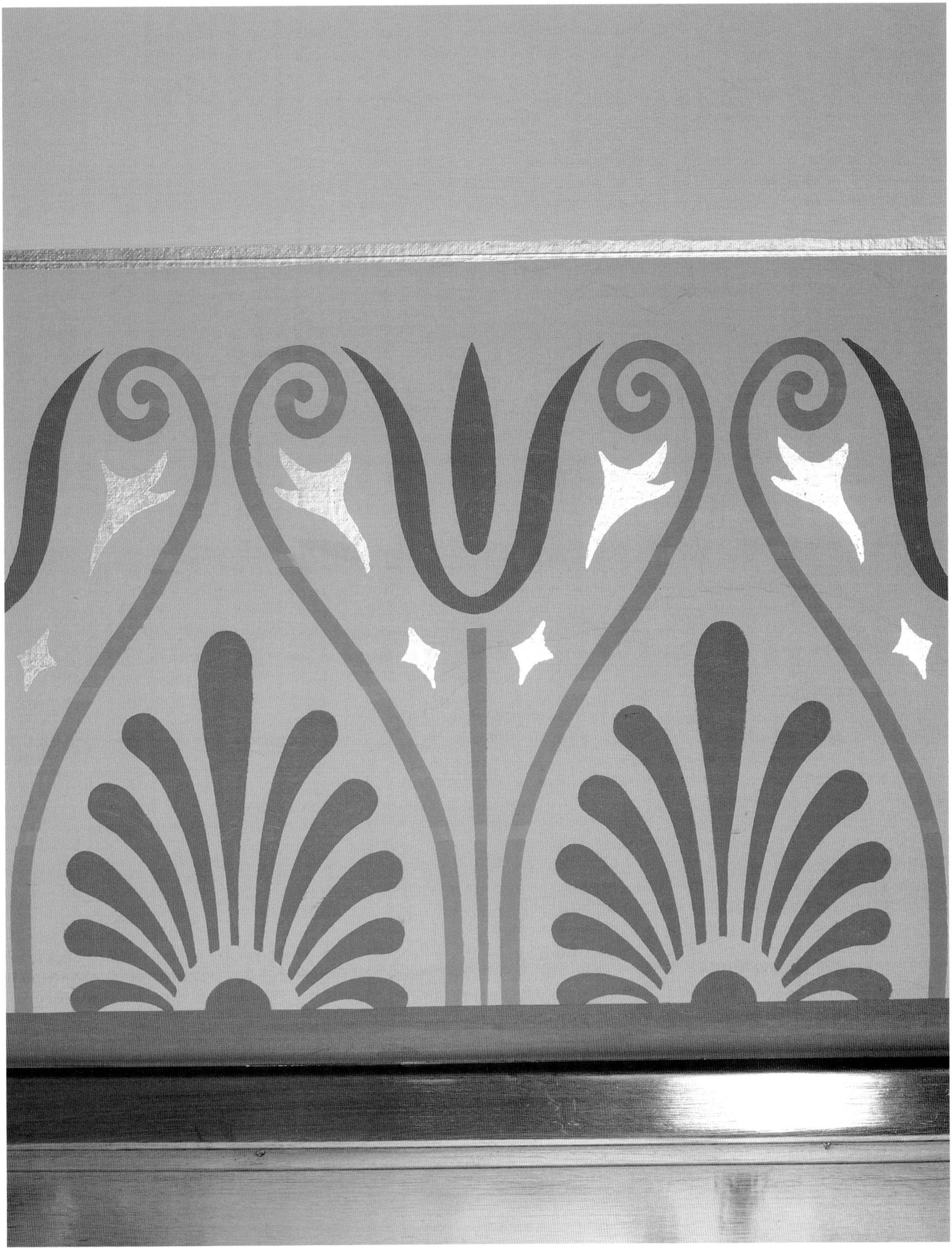

One of the lucky few to ever gain entrance to Andy Warhol's Manhattan townhouse was Pierre Bergé. Fashion editor Diana Vreeland introduced the erudite Frenchman and force behind Yves St. Laurent to Warhol and Johnson, and he was bowled over by the beauty of their townhouse. When, in 1978, Bergé purchased an apartment in New York's Pierre Hotel it was Jed Johnson he chose to supervise its decoration. Johnson was excited to have his first professional commission. In collaboration with American furniture expert Judith Hollander, and using the finest craftsmen and painters, he created one of the most celebrated apartments of its time.

The space was not large, more of a pied-à-terre, but the rooms were beautifully proportioned and the views of Central Park were splendid. Peter Marino, a Warhol Factory acquaintance, was the project architect.

The use of Egyptian Revival furniture, which had been out of fashion for three-quarters of a century, caused *Vogue* magazine to comment that the apartment had been turned into "a showcase for this period furniture such as is rarely seen in museums." Johnson's admiration for nineteenth-century stencil patterns was evident throughout. His research into the proper period designs and colors took months. The living room was painted golden beige, derived from a color in the Aubusson carpet. "One of the most beautiful things about this room" he said, "is the way the walls change tonal values in different lights." The bedroom was a richly hued terra cotta and furnished in the classical style. The stenciled friezes, the colors, and the extraordinary furnishings caused *Vogue* to pronounce that the space had "a warm, comfortable, rich ambience unlike any other in the city."

(Interior Architecture: Peter Marino; Design Assistant: Jay Johnson)

Preceding page: An early Jed Johnson trademark is the use of hand stenciling. Through most of the twentieth century it was utilized only for historic restoration, but Johnson revived the technique in the Andy Warhol townhouse. Classical acanthus and tulip motifs appears in the vestibule of the "American style" New York pied-à-terre of Pierre Bergé.

Opposite: For Pierre Bergé's entrance vestibule, Johnson found a rare Boston console table, circa 1815. It is surmounted by an 1810 gilt-wood and *églomisé* mirror and a pair of painted tole sconces, 1870. The hall chairs are New York, first quarter of the nineteenth century.

Photographs, page 31: John Hall; pages 32–41: Horst/*Vogue* © 1979 Condé Nast Publications Inc.

In the early 1850s, the first archaeological finds from Egypt toured the United States fueling a craze for Egyptian-inspired furniture. In the twentieth century only the most esoteric of collectors sought these unusual pieces. Jed Johnson and Judith Hollander found a New York-made Egyptian Revival suite of ebonized and gilt rosewood chairs and settee by Pottier and Stymus for the living room and covered them in embossed silk velvet the same golden beige color of the walls. The Egyptian Revival newel-post lamp dates from about 1870. In the background an 1860 Cornelius & Company chandelier from Philadelphia hangs above an elaborate rosewood and marquetry cabinet crafted by Gustav Herter in New York the same year. The painting is *Indian and Water Lily* by George DeForest Brush. A third-quarter nineteenth-century, New York Neo-Grec chair, with ebonized finish and ormolu mounts, sits at the edge of the Aubusson carpet.

The northern windows of the living room overlook
Central Park and are dressed in silk lampas fashioned in
a Moorish style. The Turkish suite of tufted upholstered
furniture is American from the mid-1870s, and Johnson
covered them in blue silk velvet. Leon Marcotte made the
French-style center table in New York, 1860. One of a pair
of Tiffany torchères from 1890 stands in the corner beside
a nineteenth-century portrait of an American Indian by
Charles Bird King.

An 1820s American neoclassical sleigh bed is the focal point in the bedchamber of Pierre Bergé. Covered in a French hand-loomed silk bedcover from 1810, it rests beneath the painting *Indian's Last Gaze* by Jesse Talbot, New York, 1860. The 1830 round table is by A. G. Quervelle of Philadelphia and stands on a carpet by Aubusson. Johnson painted the room a richly hued terra cotta and stenciled it with classical Greek friezes.

For the neo-Egyptian friezes in the Bergé living room, three craftsmen labored eleven weeks creating the stenciling to Johnson's specifications.

SANDRA & PETER BRANT

GREENWICH, CONNECTICUT

1982

When Jed Johnson's good friends Sandra and Peter Brant asked him to design the interiors of the grand new house being constructed at their White Birch Farm in Greenwich, Connecticut, he was overwhelmed by the prospect of such a major project, but architect Allan Greenberg designed the house, so he knew the proportions and details would be correct and beautiful. It was a new challenge.

Mr. Greenberg has recently written about their collaboration:

"In designing and decorating the interiors of a new house, it is sometimes possible to make 1+1+1 equal 4. This occurs when owner, decorator, and architect are able to collaborate and to pool their intelligence and experience. The result is a bonus: a more intense level of coordination animates both the interior architecture and the décor.

At White Birch Farm, Jed and I were blessed with amazing clients. Sandy and Peter Brant loved architecture and they had assembled a significant collection of paintings and decorative arts, modern art, and Art Deco furniture.

Jed often attended the early planning meetings. I was struck by his gentle demeanor and careful choice of words. He seemed to be aware of a tension between the words he chose and their limited ability to express his views and feelings. Observing him I recalled an old Dutch aphorism: *Stille water, dieppe grond, onder loop die duivel rond.* [Still water conceals a deep well, and underneath the devil is walking around.]

Collaboration became more intense as we moved on to studies of room elevations and decorative detail. We quickly resolved questions of the placement of registers, switches, and doors in relation to the furniture layout in each room. Observing Jed and Sandy discuss the placement of furniture and the selection of fabrics, light fixtures, carpets, and ceramics, I sensed that Jed was conceiving interiors that would be better than I imagined possible. When the house was finished, I was privileged to observe that my architecture had assumed a new aura through its dialogue with Jed's magical interiors."

(Architecture: Allan Greenberg)

Preceding page: The Brants' breakfast room at White Birch Farm is a study in plain and pure eighteenth-century American domestic decoration.

Opposite: An Ad Reinhardt black painting creates a striking contrast to the eighteenth-century appointments in the library. The brass chandelier is period as is the vivid Georgian needlework carpet.

The drawing room of Sandra and Peter Brant at White Birch Farm is illuminated by light sources from three directions. The expansive room is decorated with eighteenth-century American and English furniture. An early nineteenth-century group portrait of the Kennedy Long family by painter Joshua Johnson adds to the tone of serenity and harmony.

Right: The eighteenth-century Chinese *arboresque* fantasy wallpaper is an intense green, found in London by Johnson and Ms. Brant. The bright yellow silk damask curtains compliment Allan Greenberg's architectural details.
Overleaf: An Andy Warhol painting, *Merce*—portraits of Merce Cunningham dancing—surmounts a *galuchat blanc* cabinet by French master André Groult. The superb twentieth-century furnishings create an astonishing tableau amid the eighteenth-century-style architecture.

The sitting room is made more casual by the slipcovers of printed cotton in an eighteenth-century chinoiserie pattern. An early nineteenth-century painting, *Girl with Strawberries* by John Brewster, hangs on the wood-paneled chimneybreast. Andy Warhol's *Dick Tracy* lurks behind the door.

JED JOHNSON & ALAN WANZENBERG

NEW YORK CITY

1982

In 1980, while still residing with Andy Warhol, Jed Johnson purchased an apartment on West Sixty-seventh Street in Manhattan, a few steps from Central Park. Warhol told his diarist Pat Hackett, "He's going to use it as an office for his decorating business so his clients and all the workmen won't be tramping in and out of the house all day anymore, so that'll be a relief."

The apartment is located in a Gothic Revival building originally conceived of as studios for artists. It was designed by architects Pollard & Steinam and constructed in 1905. (An original amenity was a communal kitchen with dumb-waiter service to each unit.)

The seven-room duplex studio, which Johnson soon shared as a residence with architect Alan Wanzenberg, has a large living room with nineteen-foot ceilings and north light through a vast, double-height window. Off the main room are the library, dining room and kitchen. The balconied bedroom level overlooks the living room. The apartment features oak woodwork and, as part of the renovation, wide-plank oak floors were installed throughout except for the entry foyer where Fulper tiles were laid. A new kitchen and bath were also created. The vintage of the building and the good condition of the plain architectural details worked perfectly with Johnson's love of the furniture, art and decorative objects of the Arts & Crafts movement. "He loved the plain, clean architectural lines," says Robert Kirkland, an early design assistant. "It suited his nature and personality." It was also a good background for his collection of Warhol paintings and other contemporary art, which he liked to mix with period paintings and photography.

Johnson and Wanzenberg were able to put together an important collection of early twentieth-century English and American furniture. (Johnson is often credited with the resurgence in popularity of the Arts & Crafts style previously disdained as "old-fashioned.") The furniture, with its plain, craftsman's lines, exposed joinery, and warm oak patina was complemented with American art pottery, period lighting and carpets. The space was made fresh and modern with the colorful art.

(Interior Architecture: Alan Wanzenberg)

Preceding page: The stylized thistle motifs in the mosaic-tiled fire surround are a striking feature in the Manhattan living room of Jed Johnson and Alan Wanzenberg. Originally made for a 1901 Chicago house, the tiles were designed for architect George Washington Maher by Louis J. Millet.

Opposite: The whimsical lines of the W. A. S. Benson lamps on the oak sideboard mitigate the austerity of the furniture in the dining room. Harvey Ellis designed the round dining table and the sideboard for the Arts & Crafts master Gustav Stickley. The hanging lamp of hammered copper and molded glass is also Stickley. Stoic American Indians gaze from the pair of Edward S. Curtis photogravures.

Photographs, pages 55–67: John Hall

Presided over by a Warhol painting of Chairman Mao, the pale, cool olive-colored, double-height living room contains an impressive collection of early twentieth-century American and English furnishings. The 1915 library table by L. & J. G. Stickley supports a bronze sculpture by Mimmo Paladino and a lamp made of New England Hampshire pottery and rests on a Voysey Donegal carpet. The ladder-back chairs are by Sir Edwin Lutyens and the leather sofa is by Jed Johnson & Associates. Gustav Stickley designed the 1905 beaten-copper and glass double-lantern sconces.

A Francesco Clemente painting, *Moon,* dominates the northwest elevation of the living room. It hangs above an oak settee and a small table by Gustav Stickley, who also designed the child's rocker in the foreground. The 1920 wrought-iron standing lamp is by Addison Mizner, and the rush-seat Sussex chair flanking the settee is by the famous English firm Morris & Co.

The plain-lined dresser and side chair in the master
bedroom are Gustav Stickley as is the slatted oak rocker
reflected in the mirror. The photogravures are by Curtis.

The visual movement in the fabric covering the walls in the guest bedroom echoes the curling-vine motifs of the nineteenth-century English Gothic Revival chest. Above it hangs an anonymous nineteenth-century American painting. The bowl is from Fulper Pottery, and the candlesticks are by Christopher Dresser.

In the library a moody, mid-nineteenth-century nude by Jean-Jacques Henner reclines above the comfortably worn leather sofa. The hexagonal table is English Gothic Revival and the surrounding chairs are by the nineteenth-century, French-born American Alexander Roux. The wallpaper and the rush-seat chair were designed by William Morris.

JERRY HALL & MICK JAGGER

NEW YORK CITY

1987

In the early 1980s, when high-fashion model Jerry Hall found a five-story West Side townhouse for herself and British rock star Mick Jagger, she sought the help of Jed Johnson to cure what ailed the mixed-up, messed-up, turn-of-the-century residence. Jagger, one of the rare guests to visit Andy Warhol's East Sixty-sixth Street townhouse, was impressed with Johnson's talent as a decorator.

According to Robert Kirkland, an assistant during a portion of the project, "Jed told me the house had been converted into apartments, he thought sometime in the fifties, and it was a jumble of chopped-up rooms and added-on water closets—a nightmare of bathtubs and linoleum." Fortunately, most of the architectural detailing was intact and lay hidden behind the bad conversion. "It took months of knocking down partitions to get the place cleaned up and ready for painting," he adds. "Luckily, they were a mobile couple and did not have to live in the midst of the restoration."

Stylistically, the well-proportioned rooms varied from one to another and Johnson determined to decorate the different spaces accordingly. When the architectural portion of the project was approaching completion, he spent hours divining just the right paint colors and finishes to bring the house to life. In the French-style living room the painters used several shades of warm white and ochre to highlight the elaborate decorative plasterwork. Much research also went into the stenciled designs for the ceilings. In the library a richly hued Moorish design was applied to achieve a nineteenth-century Victorian effect, all while Johnson shopped for the proper furniture, art, and accessories to serve the needs of the high profile pair. He knew Hall's natural enjoyment of entertaining required special touches to make the place gracious, easy and hospitable. The need for privacy and security was also an important consideration.

Kirkland concludes, "Jed put together a stylish, comfortable and historically thought-out New York abode for the jet-set couple and gave them the satisfaction of a real home."

(Interior Architecture: Alan Wanzenberg; Design Associate: Robert Kirkland)

Preceding page: An austere Biedermeier cabinet bears a more fanciful nineteenth-century Chinese temple jar in the butter-yellow bedroom of Jerry Hall and Mick Jagger.

Opposite: The "French" living room has original plasterwork and marble pilasters. Johnson painted the room to highlight the fine plaster details and stenciled a delicate Greek-key frieze on the ceiling. A Louis XVI canapé flanks the elaborately carved nineteenth-century mantelpiece opposite a pair of Louis XVI Revival armchairs. The Directoire carpet is Aubusson.

The walnut paneling lends the dining room an English Arts & Crafts flavor. The Gustav Stickley table is set with nineteenth-century English ironstone plates. Johnson and Hall wanted the room dark and romantic for evening entertaining. A painting of Bacchus, god of wine and hospitality, adds a touch of color and humor.

Late nineteenth-century English tufted leather chairs add to the feeling of comfort in the library. Johnson designed a Moorish-style stenciled ceiling and included a Gothic Revival desk and glass-front bookcases. The Warhol dollar-sign painting lends a playful note.

IRJA & JEFFREY STEINER

NEW YORK CITY

1988

According to Arthur Dunnam, the Irja and Jeffrey Steiner project in New York was the first job for Jed Johnson "outside the Andy Warhol network of friends and acquaintances." It was an important moment when Johnson's own reputation as a designer began to attract clients solely for the beauty and quality of his work. It was to be the first of ten subsequent projects of varying sizes and scopes for the Steiners and their immediate family.

A major part of the assignment was the editing of the clients' own English and French furniture. The international businessman and his Swedish wife owned a broad range from the seventeenth through the nineteenth centuries. Johnson assessed the appropriateness of each piece in juxtaposition with their impressive collection of European art. "If it didn't work for New York," Dunnam says, "it would be shipped to their sprawling villa in St. Tropez for possible use elsewhere."

Dimitri Balamotis's designs for the architectural renovation of the large Fifth Avenue apartment were well under way when Johnson received his commission. "We found an incredible period Robert Adam chimneypiece for the living room and made a few minor modifications to Dimitri's beautiful plans," Dunnam explains. "It was a productive collaboration."

The decoration reflected the European tastes of the clients, with mahogany paneling in the entry gallery and rich paint finishes throughout. Johnson's serene color palette and use of luxurious textiles created a subtle environment of great quality and depth.

(Interior Architecture: Dimitri Balamotis; Design Associate: Arthur Dunnam)

Preceding page: A child plays on the beach in the Maurice Denis painting hanging above the carved and inlaid Robert Adam chimneypiece, in the Manhattan living room of Irja and Jeffrey Steiner.

Opposite: A chinoiserie figure sits calmly atop one of a pair of highly ornate George III gilt-wood looking glasses in the dining room. An early nineteenth-century Russian chandelier is reflected in the mirror. Hand-painted eighteenth-century Chinese wallpaper lines the room.

Photographs, pages 77–85: Michael Mundy

A nineteenth-century Indian Agra carpet anchors the living
room, where a period Régence *bureau plat* rests between
the windows flanked by a pair of giltwood Régence *bergères*.
The room boasts a fine collection of seventeenth- and
eighteenth-century French furniture. A Mary Cassatt pastel
hangs above an ormolu-mounted commode.

Left: The rich mahogany-paneled entry gallery contains a
Directoire center table of bronze, gilt bronze, and marble.
A nineteenth-century marble dish lamp is suspended overhead,
and a painting by Marc Chagall hangs in the hallway beyond.
Overleaf: The wood-paneled walls of the living room are glazed
with a creamy strié finish. The sofa is flanked by an important
pair of Régence beechwood side tables and Louis XV gilt-wood
fauteuils. George II gilt-wood brackets support eighteenth-
century Chinese "nodding head" figures. The table is a Jed
Johnson & Associates design in the style of the French Directoire
period. The painting is *Uncle Benny's Dune* by Childe Hassam.

GLENN DUBIN

NEW YORK CITY

1992

The businessman Glenn Dubin and Jed Johnson had much in common. Both appreciated art and furniture of the mid-twentieth century, and both loved French design. It was only natural that when these two friends became client and designer, a modernist, Parisian-style apartment would evolve. "Jed had the uncanny ability to be ahead of his time," says Arthur Dunnam, the associate designer on the project. "During the popular rediscovery of Art Deco in the 1980s, Jed, who had long utilized the furniture and designs of Dunand and Ruhlmann, was already focusing his eye on the French modernists of the 1940s and 1950s. Royère, Prouvé, and Roche were appearing in Jed's work as frequently as the more generally known masters of the prior decades."

Dubin already lived in the well-proportioned apartment and expressed no urgency during the acquisition process. His frequent business trips to Paris often coincided with Johnson's shopping trips, so the two could make the rounds of dealers' galleries together, choosing each piece for its appropriateness as well as its beauty.

The apartment, though a sound prewar space, was plain in its architecture. Johnson decided to create a simple yet glamorous nighttime background for his client's collection of art, furniture, and objects. He began with wall surfaces of pewter-leaf tea paper for the living room, a geometric stencil pattern for the entry foyer, and a faux-tortoise glaze over the existing orange color for the dining room. The subtle tones provided a warm glow, rich but not overdone.

Architecturally, the pièce de résistance was a gold-veined black marble mantelpiece in the style of Émile-Jacques Ruhlmann, which formed a stunning modernist focal point for the living room.

(Design Associate: Arthur Dunnam)

Preceding page: A painting by Francesco Clemente hangs on the pewter tea paper-covered walls in the living room of Manhattanite Glenn Dubin. Franz Hagenauer silver figures box on the Jean Royère coffee table. Johnson was a pioneer in the rediscovery of the 1940s French designers.

Opposite: In the bedroom a nineteenth-century French recamier rests in front of a mahogany and glass Russian screen. The gilt-bronze sconce is by Jules Leleu.

The foyer walls are hand-stenciled in a contemporary, geometric design. On the 1940s French console rest a pair of 1920s Sèvres vases. Through to the living room, a Royère metal and leather game table and chairs stand on the edge of a custom-designed Aubusson carpet by Jed Johnson & Associates. The standing lamp is Royère as well.

In the living room a Mimmo Paladino painting hangs above
an Émile-Jacques Ruhlmann chair. Jed Johnson & Associates
designed the Ruhlmann-inspired chimneypiece. Above it
hangs a 1940 leather mirror by Serge Roche. A painted
ceramic urn by Peter Schlesinger rests between the windows.
The room is trimmed in ebonized mahogany.

The luster of the tortoiseshell-glazed walls gives a dramatic glow to the dining room. The Robert Cassilly tinted concrete bas-relief baboons watch passively, flanked by Royère-inspired torchères. The gilt-wood, continental chandelier is nineteenth century. The limed oak table is crafted in the style of Jean-Michel Frank.

MAUREEN & MARSHALL COGAN

NEW YORK CITY

1993

In 1991, to complement their fine collection of modern master art, Maureen and Marshall Cogan turned for assistance to Jed Johnson and Alan Wanzenberg who had, by then, gained a reputation for the quiet luxury and elegance of their design collaborations. The apartment, overlooking the treetops of New York's Central Park, became a twentieth-century classic with sensitively rescaled proportions, satinwood paneling, parchment and silk wall coverings, and subtle details.

"Mrs. Cogan loves the process," says Buzz Kelly, Johnson's associate on the project. "She enjoys the collaboration and the discovery." The process led to the purchase of extraordinary French furniture by the great twentieth-century makers Jacques-Émile Ruhlmann, Jean-Michel Frank, Jean Royère, and others. "Despite the iconic art and furniture, the rooms are relaxed and comfortable and devoid of pretension," Mr. Kelly adds.

Of one of their early expeditions, Mrs. Cogan writes: "Jed and I were in Paris shopping for furniture. He identified each designer, knew the proportions we needed, explained to me where each piece would go. He was creating rooms in his head. . . . Finally, he pulled—from the bottom of some pile in a dingy, dark basement—a silver chandelier . . . he was beaming and triumphant." The chandelier was restored and hung in the entrance hall of the apartment. "It was gorgeous," she continues. "Then I understood that what he did was not always so obvious and easy."

(Interior Architecture: Alan Wanzenberg; Project Architect: Alexander Antonelli; Design Associate: Buzz Kelly)

Preceding page: A Paul Klee painting hangs above a 1940s console by Jean Royère in the Manhattan home of Maureen and Marshall Cogan. A Henry Moore bronze figure sits serenely amid Jed Johnson's luxurious homage to twentieth-century art and modernism.

Opposite: Square parchment panels cover the walls of the dining room, where a nineteenth-century Russian chandelier is suspended above a table crafted in the style of Émile-Jacques Ruhlmann. Around the table are early nineteenth-century Russian chairs. The paintings are by the Italian Futurists Giacomo Balla and Gino Severini. The silk curtains disappear discreetly within pockets in the window reveal, a feature repeated throughout the apartment.

Left: An Alberto Giacometti bronze figure stands guard in the Cogan living room, which is decorated with treasures from twentieth-century French artists and furniture makers. A 1935 painting by Miró hangs above a shagreen and macassar ebony chest by Jean-Michel Frank. The round table standing before the fireplace is by the Art Deco master Ruhlmann, as are the silver sconces and the upholstered, lacquer-armed lounge chair. The low table of shagreen and ebony is also Frank. Paintings by Picasso and Léger grace the fireplace wall. A Marion Dorn carpet gives weight to the room and unifies the collection.

Overleaf: The satinwood-paneled entrance gallery sets the mood for the entire apartment, a tribute to modernism. The silver and alabaster sconces by Ruhlmann illuminate a portrait by Francis Bacon. The metal-edged door and window reveals provide a rich but tailored effect throughout the residence.

Preceding page: The bathroom, fitted with early twentieth-century fixtures, is paneled in satinwood with floors of marble mosaic. Above hangs a nineteenth-century alabaster lamp. That master of modernism Jean-Michel Frank designed the dressing-table stool.

Right: The clean lines of a *bureau plat*, stamped Philippe-Claude Montigny, 1766, easily blend with the twentieth-century architecture and objects in the library. Upon the desk rests a modernist lamp by Diego Giacometti, demonstrating Johnson's fondness for mixing compatible pieces from any period. The smartly tailored satinwood paneling is repeated from the entrance gallery, and the classically modern plaster cornice runs throughout the apartment. The low tables are by Jean-Michel Frank, including the round table of straw marquetry beside a comfortable chair and ottoman. A bronze panther by Rembrandt Bugatti stalks behind the Frank sofa. A 1908 Picasso drawing and a 1949 painting by Léger share an ample corner. The serene beauty of the room is magically juxtaposed with the dazzling view of the New York skyline and Central Park.

STEPHANIE & CARTER MCCLELLAND

NEW YORK CITY

1993

When Stephanie and Carter McClelland moved their family to a large apartment in one of the premier buildings on Central Park West they knew they would need help with the long-neglected infrastructure of the five-thousand-square-foot space. Friends put them in touch with Jed Johnson and Alan Wanzenberg. What began as a small renovation and new kitchen gradually grew into a major design project as the couple came to know and respect the understated decorator and his architect partner.

Johnson guided the direction of the design toward what might be called traditional modernism. His love for the great French designers of the mid-twentieth century was his inspiration. He assigned associates Vance Burke and Buzz Kelly to assist with the project and slowly a sumptuous space with surfaces of fine brass-inlaid wood, parchment and lacquer emerged.

"The McClellands collected fine furniture as avidly as they had fine paintings," recalls Burke. "She had been an executive who left the business world to raise a family. Her organizational skills were remarkable." The newly detailed rooms of the subtlest richness became the perfect showcase for the clients' collection of modern and contemporary art. Johnson's exacting eye for detail, correct scale and sophisticated color palette completed the vision. The results were a superb Jed Johnson mix of art, objects, and furniture perfectly suited to each other and to the lifestyle of the clients.

(Interior Architecture: Alan Wanzenberg; Project Architect: Timothy Joslin; Design Associates: Vance Burke and Buzz Kelly)

Preceding page: The Art Deco-inspired bed, chest, and cabinet (reflected in the gilt mirror in the style of Jean-Michel Frank) were designed by Jed Johnson & Associates for the apartment of Stephanie and Carter McClelland. Mrs. McClelland's favorite color, red, is used on an upholstered chaise lounge. Beside it rests a nineteenth-century Chinese *sang de boeuf* lamp. The walls are upholstered in a French silk Jacquard.

Opposite: Classic modernism is evoked in the dining room, where a Caio Fonseca painting hangs on parchment-paneled walls. An English Regency table and chairs mix perfectly with mid-twentieth-century elements.

Photographs, pages 107–15: Scott Frances, originally published in *Architectural Digest*

Preceding pages: Johnson specified sixteen coats of Chinese red lacquer for the walls of the entrance gallery, where a graceful 1840s English settee sits across from a pair of twentieth-century Emilio Thierry consoles. The large abstract painting by Joan Mitchell is titled *Sunday, August 12, 1956.*
Right: A vast nineteenth-century Ziegler Sultanabad carpet anchors the living room, where a Franz Kline work hangs between the windows. A pair of Italian, mid-century Lucite and bronze obelisks and a painting by Joan Mitchell rest on a black lacquer 1940s cabinet by Jacques Quinet. The horsehair-covered benches are by Jacques Adnet, and the open armchair is nineteenth-century Swedish.

Across the living room a grand piano—which once belonged to Leonard Bernstein—waits to be played beneath a 1994 painting by Helmut Dorner. To the right, a pair of 1940s French chairs, upholstered in leather, flank a Russian neoclassical table in the cream-colored, sun-filled salon.

MARILYN & SAM FOX

SAINT LOUIS, MISSOURI

1994

"Jed was fortunate to work with a number of talented architects during his career," Arthur Dunnam states. "One of the finest was Hugh Newell Jacobsen." The project he refers to is the 14,000-square-foot addition to the home of the business executive Sam Fox and his wife, Marilyn. The Saint Louis couple interviewed an array of interior designers before choosing Jed Johnson to supervise the vast undertaking. Working in collaboration with Jacobsen and the architect Scott Weaver of Alan Wanzenberg's office, Johnson created what Dunnam describes as "the apotheosis of a period recreation, with no detail overlooked."

Except for the period furnishings and antique architectural elements, every component was custom designed for the house. Artisans were flown in from New York and elsewhere to practice their special crafts. The artist James Boyd was in Saint Louis for months executing the meticulous stencil designs. Recalling Johnson's "calm perfectionism," Boyd says, "He brought a seriousness of interest and intent that he shared with all the craftspeople on a job in a spirit of collaboration and respect that elicited our best work." He adds, "This collegial attitude was key to achieving quality and enjoying its pursuit."

This pursuit of quality was the foremost consideration for the Foxes, who, with Johnson, purchased extraordinary eighteenth-century English and continental furniture, carpets, and objects. When the three-year collaboration had finished, the result was what Dunnam calls "the exuberance and highly decorative whimsy of Tudor Gothic, tempered with the elegance of Georgian furniture and detail."

(Architecture: Hugh Newell Jacobsen; Interior Architecture: J. Scott Weaver; Design Associate: Arthur Dunnam)

Preceding page: A bronze and glass door panel designed by Jed Johnson & Associates for the home of Marilyn and Sam Fox.

Opposite: An eighteenth-century English tall-case clock stands against faux limestone-painted walls in an octagonal, Gothic-vaulted anteroom. In the stair hall beyond, the Gothic-style railing and entry door were custom designed by Jed Johnson & Associates.

Photographs, pages 117–27: John Hall

The living room is appointed with eighteenth-century English furniture. The carpet is a period-detailed, custom-designed needlepoint. Above it is suspended a nineteenth-century French gilt-bronze and rock-crystal chandelier.

The dining room is walnut paneled. An eighteenth-century Irish crystal chandelier hangs from the custom-designed plaster strapwork ceiling. The triple-pedestal dining table is George III. Wool and silk damask designed by A. W. Pugin covers the George II chairs. The mid-nineteenth-century Gothic Revival chimneypiece is limestone with inlaid marble.

Left: Gothic fretwork *verre églomisé* panels are set into the mahogany woodwork of the intimate telephone room off the entry foyer. On the limestone and marble inlaid floor stands an 1880s Gothic Revival side chair.

Overleaf, left: The walls of the library are clad in Gothic-style cherry-wood paneling. The hand-stenciled ceiling in pomegranate, leaf, and vine motifs, illuminated with gold leaf, reflects the colors of the mid-nineteenth-century French needlepoint carpet. In the background a George II mirror, one of a pair, surmounts a fine George I gilt gesso console, also one of a pair.

Overleaf, right: A chinoiserie, lacquered canopy bed dominates a guest bedroom of dark English oak paneling. Arts & Crafts painted and glazed tiles are incorporated in the fire surround. The custom-trimmed bed hangings and the curtains are crafted of French warp-printed silk rep. The bedcover is hand-embroidered crewelwork in an eighteenth-century English palampore-inspired design.

BARBARALEE DIAMONSTEIN & CARL SPIELVOGEL

SOUTHAMPTON, NEW YORK

1994

When Barbaralee Diamonstein and husband Carl Spielvogel purchased their Southampton, Long Island, house the interiors had no architectural style. Built in 1895, the once grand, Shingle Style, oceanside mansion had suffered years of neglect and inappropriate additions. Calling it Bonnie Dune, its long forgotten original name, they went to work. Diamonstein, the well-known historic preservationist and arts advocate, enlisted architects Samuel White and Michael Dwyer of Buttrick White & Burtis to completely rebuild the house, and she commissioned Jed Johnson to restore the interiors. In a close designer-client collaboration, a stately yet comfortable residence evolved, incorporating period furniture, hand-crafted interior details, decorative objects, and marine motifs.

"Jed had a regard for historical references and a very pure eye," says Diamonstein. "Despite his reserved demeanor, he had an informed point of view and the willingness to share it, much like Carl. That is why they got on so well, and that is why the entire process was a pleasing and tranquil exchange," she continues. "We all loved the give and take."

Under Johnson's supervision and Diamonstein's scholarship, the interiors of the house became as elaborately detailed as the elegant exterior. Architectural elements were added in the vocabulary of Stanford White, who was possibly the original architect. They made use of research into White's seaside cottage interiors, as well as a degree of creative interpretation. One of the most decorative and fanciful rooms is a powder room encrusted with seashells (see page 13). It is not the typical Rococo confection but rather an ordered geometry of shells that blend into the structure with dignity and restraint.

Diamonstein concludes, "What made Jed's work so interesting was that it ultimately revealed something about Jed's interior—his complexity, mystery, and sensibility."

(Architecture: Buttrick White & Burtis; Project Architect: Michael Dwyer; Interior Architecture: Alan Wazenberg; Project Architect (Interiors): Scott Cornelius; Design Associate: Arthur Dunnam)

Preceding page: An English Regency convex mirror reflects a Dale Chihuly ceiling sculpture in the entry stair hall of Bonnie Dune, the oceanside house of Barbaralee Diamonstein and Carl Spielvogel. Examples of Diamonstein's extensive collection of Palissy ware enliven the eighteenth-century English *grisaille* console. The custom-made beadboard walls are of heroic scale.

Opposite: In the subtly hued, green dining room, an unusual 1920s Scandinavian chinoiserie chandelier with scallop-shell motifs is suspended above. George III mahogany chairs surround the table, which is set with vintage green glassware and an assortment of majolica tazzos with aquatic motifs.

The hand-hooked carpet of massive size anchors the living room. An assortment of tufted Victorian chairs, covered in white crewelwork, stand in front of the original mantelpiece with redesigned fire surround of aquatic-motif tiles. All other architectural detailing is newly designed. The lacquer commode and mirror were designed by Jed Johnson & Associates.

The library is accented with numerous pieces of majolica from Diamonstein's collection. The fire surround is custom designed with bas-relief motifs of sea creatures. The nineteenth-century sofa and chairs are upholstered in hand-embroidered cotton.

Several third-floor rooms were sacrificed to create the impressive double-height master suite with its perfectly proportioned, new Palladian window. The tufted recamiers are nineteenth century, and the hand-hooked rugs are early twentieth-century American. The painted four-poster bed was custom designed by Jed Johnson & Associates.

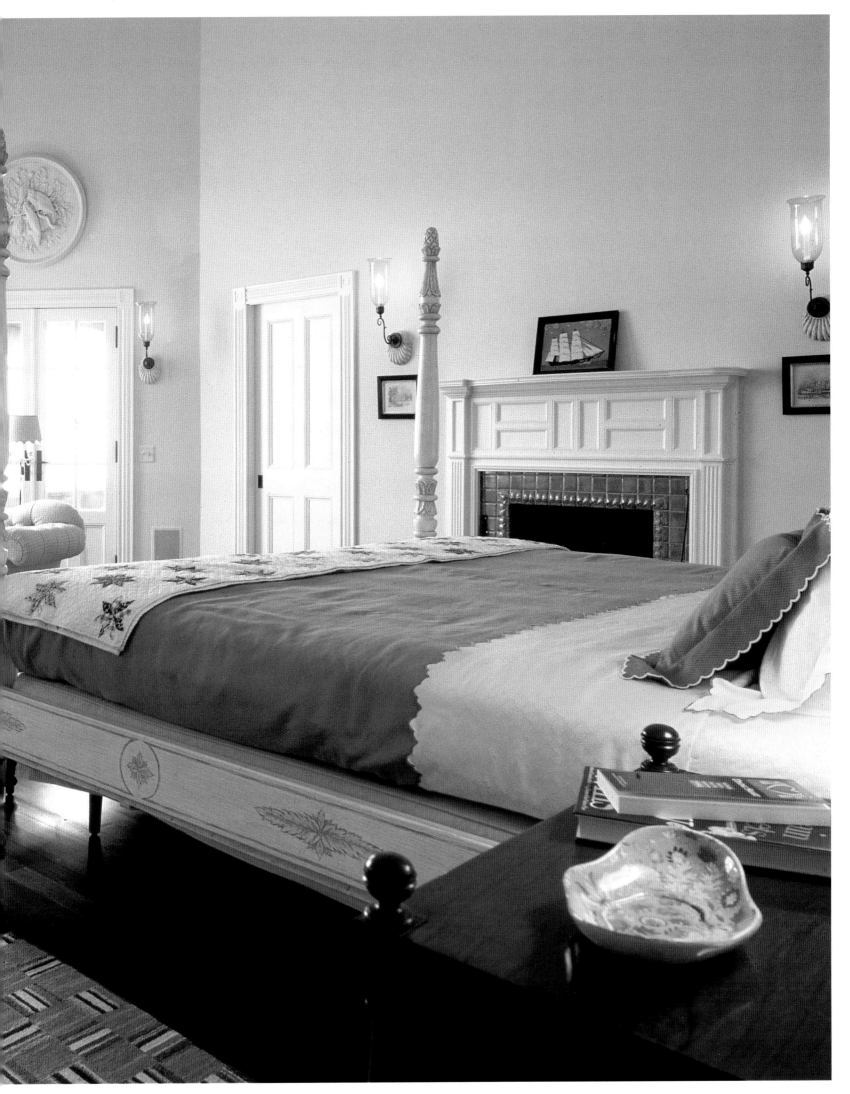

TWIN FARMS

BARNARD, VERMONT

1995

In 1928 the writer Sinclair Lewis and his new wife, the journalist Dorothy Thompson, purchased a 1795 farmhouse in Barnard, Vermont. They named it Twin Farms, and the house and its two large parcels of property became their retreat from the hectic New York scene and a haven for their friends, the literati and artists of the 1930s. The Lewises constructed a connecting passage between the house and the barn, which stood across a side yard, creating a spacious studio for work and entertaining.

Six decades later another couple, Laila and Thurston Twigg-Smith, purchased Twin Farms for their country getaway. They soon found it logistically impractical as a second home, because their primary residence was in Honolulu. After the initial disappointment of not being able to spend enough time in the idyllic landscape and charming house, they decided to turn the dwelling and its 235 acres into a deluxe, rustic resort that could be enjoyed year-round by fortunate guests.

After scouring design literature, Mrs. Twigg-Smith contacted Jed Johnson & Associates and soon interviewed Johnson and Alan Wanzenberg. "They say that opposites attract," says Vance Burke, a design associate on the project. "Laila and Jed became instant friends. His quiet nature and restrained sensibility clicked with her outgoing personality and extravagant tastes. They enjoyed learning from each other."

The master plan was to restore the main house and to construct a series of guest cottages, each unique yet all sensitive to the natural terrain. Time had taken its toll on the house. "None of the walls was true," Burke explains. "Basically, it all had to be taken apart and put back together." The main house and eventually eight cottages were completed carefully and gradually. In a relatively short time Twin Farms became a legendary holiday destination for guests from around the world.

(Architecture: Alan Wanzenberg; Project Architect: Scott Cornelius; Design Associates: Vance Burke, Buzz Kelly, and Andy Clark)

Preceding page: The final glow of twilight reflected on the snow of Vermont is seen through a great window at the end of the old barn at Twin Farms. Jed Johnson and Alan Wanzenberg were asked to turn the former country home of Sinclair Lewis and Dorothy Thompson into a luxurious resort while maintaining the authentic New England charm.

Opposite: The main entry hall is contained in the original passage built by Lewis and Thompson to connect the main house with the barn. Johnson commissioned the muralist James Boyd to paint a naive country scene on the plaster walls. A New England pinecone mirror topped with deer antlers surmounts a nineteenth-century rustic French chest. Above hangs an antique French brass-and-mirror ceiling lantern.

Photographs, pages 139–58: John Hall

The Perch Cottage dressing room provides a touch of humor.
An English Arts & Crafts brass lantern lights the hand-painted
aquatic frieze by James Boyd. In the bathroom beyond, a
restored antique copper bathtub gleams.

Left: A large, custom-braided wool carpet warms the floor of the Perch Cottage, which is accented with aquatic elements. Antique lures, gigs, and fishmonger signage cover the wall above the dining corner where an English gate-leg table and Windsor-back chairs rest.

Overleaf: Positioned on a hillside at treetop level, the Treehouse was designed with a fretwork of white-birch ceiling beams. The custom-made twisted bedposts terminate in hand-carved ravens.

Preceding page: In the Log Cabin a dramatic nineteenth-century French chandelier with dog-head motifs emblazons the rafters. The English Edwardian chair with dog-head hand rests is upholstered in a nineteenth-century American quilt. The Adirondack-style bench is covered in an antique blanket.

Right: The walls and furnishings in a guest room of the main house are covered in an early nineteenth-century French toile de Jouy design depicting the heroic arrival of Lafayette in America. The wool and sisal plaid carpet was specially woven for the room. An early twentieth-century bronze Native American lamp stands on a barley twist table.

The Washington Room of the main house is decorated with
American folk art, rag rugs, and hand-stenciled walls.

Left: A hand-woven ash ceiling from Kyoto and hay-rubbed plaster walls create a distinctively exotic look in the bedroom of Orchard Cottage. Sliding checkerboard ash-wood panels control the natural light. In the foreground stands an Indian fireside chair, and beyond the bed lean two tall ladders from Africa. *Overleaf, left and right:* The exterior of Meadow Cottage is vernacular country New England in its architecture. The surprise interiors are pure Moroccan-inspired fantasy. The tent-shaped, striped plaster ceilings are adorned with lanterns from Marrakech. Mosaic tilework and hand stenciling ornament the raised seating area of the bedroom.

Right: The double-height sitting room of the Studio Cottage holds a comfortable mix of modern, contemporary, and country furnishings. From the spatter-painted floor to the custom-designed Bob Russell chandelier, the spirit of an artist's studio is evoked. A Mexican bark-paper screen stands beneath the high window and behind a nineteenth-century painted farm table; a pair of 1940s French leather ottomans nestle underneath. The free-form lacquered coffee table was custom designed for the space. David Hockney works on paper adorn the wall.

The furniture and iron chandeliers in the dining room were
designed by Jed Johnson & Associates, as was the
checkerboard, braided-wool carpet. A Boyd-Reath Studio
hand-stenciled, oakleaf-patterned frieze surrounds the room.
The crane painting is by David Bates.

BROOKE & DANIEL NEIDICH

NEW YORK CITY

1996

"Jed was very excited by how the Neidich apartment turned out," says Christine Cain, who worked on the project with him. "He loved its subdued modernism and said he would like to work more often in the same aesthetic for other clients."

In 1994 Brooke and Daniel Neidich purchased a roomy apartment in an East Side Manhattan building, constructed in the 1930s by Vincent Astor. The rooms were spacious and well proportioned but needed to function better for a modern couple with children. The Neidichs sought the assistance of Jed Johnson and Alan Wanzenberg to reconfigure the architecture and design the interiors. "Brooke is so stylish and free-thinking," Cain states. "She was open to any idea or suggestion Jed might propose."

Major construction was undertaken not only to modernize the infrastructure but also to realign spaces to take better advantage of the views. "A limestone fireplace, inspired by Jean-Michel Frank, was installed in the living room to replace a much larger one that Jed felt overpowered the room," adds Cain.

The room was given "silky-smooth paint finishes in shades of creamy beige that change in tone with the changing light," Cain describes. To maintain the airy, open quality he desired, Johnson recommended furniture on legs and skirtless upholstered pieces. Most of the furniture throughout is mid-twentieth-century French, with elegant suites by Jansen providing seating in the living room and library.

"The restrained opulence provided by Jed's guidance and connoisseurship created a luminous background for art," Cain concludes, "and a comfortable place to raise a family."

(Interior Architecture: Alan Wanzenberg; Project Architect: Timothy Joslin; Design Associate: Christine Cain)

Preceding page: In 1995 Johnson went into partnership with the London textile dealer Mona Perlhagen to create the New York-based company Chelsea Editions. Once again he was ahead of the crowd. Their seventeenth- and eighteenth-century documentary designs repopularized hand-embroidered home-furnishing fabrics in America and spilled over into apparel design as well. For Brooke and Daniel Neidich he used "Eighteenth-Century Vine" on a custom-designed, blackened-steel tester bed.

Opposite: A Jean-Michel Frank–inspired limestone mantelpiece is centered in the living room. The French gilt-bronze sconces are inset with shagreen backplates.

Photographs, pages 161–67: François Halard, originally published in *House & Garden*

The library contains a suite of serpentine-front, leather-upholstered furniture by the great French design house Jansen. A painting by Caio Fonseca surmounts the fireplace. The wood cabinet to the left is a Jed Johnson & Associates design.

A Julian Schnabel collage presides over the Neidichs'
light-filled living room. The 1940s French library table
holds a collection of Venini glass. The sofa and chair are
part of a suite by Jansen.

MAUREEN & MARSHALL COGAN

SOUTHAMPTON, NEW YORK

1996

"As stimulating and inspiring as art is," says designer Vance Burke, "the absence of art can inspire a mood of relaxation and introspection. I think that's what the Cogans had in mind when they discussed the design of the Southampton house with Jed." The art-filled Manhattan apartment of Maureen and Marshall Cogan (see pages 96–105) seems a world away from the simple decoration and virtually art-free environment of their Long Island country house. The contrast is striking. "Jed was all about editing," continues Burke, an associate on the project. "His natural inclination was that less is better."

Architecturally, the early twentieth-century Shingle Style house needed only minor adjustments to unify the space as a whole. This was accomplished in part by converting an awkward passageway from the living room to the dining room into a comfortable seating area, with a new fireplace design that matches others on the main-floor level. The walls were painted white throughout.

"Mrs. Cogan wanted things Swedish," says Buzz Kelly, who also worked on the project. "Of course, that pleased Jed enormously. He loved the simple lines and painted finishes of Gustavian furniture. Perhaps it spoke to his Scandinavian roots."

The final result was a serene and worry-free summer gathering place for the entire Cogan family, including grown children and grandchildren. "If you told people you were decorating a house with no art and no color they might be taken aback," continues Kelly. "Jed could make simplicity a beautiful object in and of itself."

(Interior Architecture: Alan Wanzenberg; Project Architect: Alex Antonelli; Design Associates: Vance Burke and Buzz Kelly)

Preceding page: The simplicity of eighteenth- and nineteenth-century Swedish furniture adds grace to the country home of Maureen and Marshall Cogan, where slipcovers, wicker, and sisal strike a contrast with the couple's high-style Manhattan apartment.

Opposite: A sitting room connects the living room to the more formal dining room. Alan Wanzenberg reconfigured the flow of the spaces. The Swedish console table, one of a pair, is eighteenth century.

Photographs, pages 169–77: Scott Frances, originally published in *Architectural Digest*

A painted antique wicker chair blends with occasional tables by the designer Christian Astuguevieille in the living room, made for easy weekend entertaining. The diamond-front chest is eighteenth-century Swedish.

Left: Two of the dining room chairs are eighteenth-century Swedish. The rest were perfectly duplicated by Jed Johnson & Associates. The cabinet, one of a pair, is eighteenth-century as well. Johnson located the nineteenth-century American chandelier, originally made for a sailing vessel, in Paris. The table was custom designed for the room. *Overleaf:* Painted wicker furniture and antique wire planters ornament the long, comfortable veranda.

KATHERINE BRISTOR & WILLIAM PRIEST

NEW YORK CITY

1996

"Bill Priest had a true affinity for fine English furniture of the late eighteenth century," recalls Marcy Masterson, Johnson's associate on the Fifth Avenue design project that the financier commissioned for himself and his soon-to-be wife, the lawyer Katherine Bristor. "The apartment became an Anglophile's dream."

The two-year experience began with a recommendation from a real-estate broker who was acquainted with the designer and his work. "Jed was always so kind and courteous and quietly glamorous, people fell all over themselves to recommend him for jobs," adds Masterson.

"Jed had received so much press and publicity for the Arts & Crafts work he did, many people didn't realize his versatility," she continues. "He truly loved the best of every period and was delighted by this opportunity to work with good, brown English furniture."

The color palette was determined by the hues in a bucolic nineteenth-century painting by Henri Martin that was already owned by the client. The living room became a "braised celery" tone. The large Fereghan carpet anchored the spacious park-view salon. "Mr. Priest was so often in London on business he could visit dealers to see appropriate pieces we had previously scouted," remembers Masterson. "He enjoyed the collaboration."

The most extraordinary acquisition for the apartment was the eighteenth-century Chinese scenic wallpaper depicting a whole village of houses and figures, all in tones of green and brown, a gift from Emperor Ch'ien Lung to the Earl of Leicester. The paper had never been installed until Johnson found it for the dining room. "It fit almost perfectly," Masterson states. "It was a real coup."

(Interior Architecture: Alan Wanzenberg; Project Architect: Timothy Joslin; Design Associates: Marcy Masterson and Andy Clark)

Preceding page: The entry gallery, viewed from the library, in the home of Katherine Bristor and William Priest shows one of a pair of George III gilt-wood mirrors surmounting an eighteenth-century marquetry demi-lune console, also one of a pair.

Opposite: An early twentieth-century French tole chandelier hangs in the breakfast room above a cherry-wood table designed by Jed Johnson & Associates. The floor is of encaustic tile. A hand-stenciled all-over pattern brings subtle depth to the walls.

Photographs, pages 179–87: John Hall

Rare George III bookcases flank a living room view of
Central Park and display a collection of *famille vert* Chinese
porcelain. Regency corner chairs attend the eighteenth-
century English oval partners' desk. The original petit point
tapestry ornaments the gilt-wood Gainsborough chair,
which is one of a pair in the room. The large carpet is a
nineteenth-century Fereghan.

The superb eighteenth-century Chinese figurative wallpaper was originally a gift of the Emperor Ch'ien Lung to the Earl of Leicester. "It had never been installed," says Marcy Masterson, the design associate on the project, "and it fit almost perfectly. Only a small strip had to be hand painted to match." The Georgian furniture rests on a late nineteenth-century Fereghan Mustaphi carpet.

In the master bedroom the coverlet is made of eighteenth-century embroidered motifs removed from the original ground and resewn onto antique linen. The bed-hangings are of embossed wool lined with hand embroidery. A Chippendale chest of drawers and a George III bedside commode, both circa 1770, flank the bed.

ANGELA WESTWATER & DAVID MEITUS

NEW YORK CITY

1996

Designing an interior for one of America's premier art dealers and her husband provides a special set of conditions: the utmost respect for and knowledge of art and the best and most appropriate combination of art and environment. Thus, the renowned dealer Angela Westwater of the Sperone-Westwater Gallery and David Meitus, who owns a showroom serving architects and designers, chose Jed Johnson to design their Manhattan apartment. Westwater recalls, "Jed knew about art—it was part of his vocabulary. The restraint which characterized his design aesthetic combined with his personal experience in the art world were appropriate attributes for creating a context for our art collection. . . . He understood the essentials, including simplicity and suitability, for providing a background where art would be the focus."

The sequence of rooms and the large spaces of the pre-war Fifth Avenue co-operative, were perfect for the combined Westwater and Meitus collections, instantly attracting the couple to the apartment. They asked Alan Wanzenberg to design the interior architecture; they had worked with Johnson and him on previous projects.

"Particularly impressive, and refined, was Jed's great sense of color," explains Meitus. "The slight, subtle progression of colors from entrance vestibule into the larger central gallery, thence to the living room, dining room, and library reveals his nuanced palette, which contributed to such successful, gracious, and elegant interiors."

Addressing Johnson's restraint, he continues, "Jed knew when to stop. When it was suggested that we might gold leaf the vaulted ceiling of the entrance vestibule, he merely smiled, and in his soft-spoken voice suggested that that might be too much. As quiet as Jed's voice was, when he spoke we listened, and we always learned."

(Interior Architecture: Alan Wanzenberg; Project Architect: Donald Cantillo; Design Associate: Christine Cain)

Preceding page: The warm glow of a mid-twentieth-century French, etched-glass lantern casts diamond shadows across the walls and vaulted ceiling of the entrance vestibule to the Fifth Avenue apartment of Angela Westwater and David Meitus. Through the wide gallery beyond, a Susan Rothenberg horse painting is seen in the couple's library.

Opposite: Johnson and Meitus nixed the initial idea of embossed leather walls for his study and opted to commission a mural by Jane Kaplowitz. The effect is grandly subtle. A Rob Wynne collage and a Susan Rothenberg drawing hang above a pair of African tribal hats. To the right a Navajo mask stares hauntingly, supported on a pedestal by Carlo Bugatti.

Photographs, pages 189–97: Thiebault Jeanson, originally published in *House & Garden*

Left: The Westwater-Meitus art collection was the primary consideration when Johnson received the design commission. The living room is an elegant and subdued background for works by Mimmo Paladino, Gerhard Richter, and Francesco Clemente (seen here left to right). Ancient heads gazing silently from the marble mantelpiece and around the room echo imagery in the paintings and add to the mood of serenity. The circular *verre églomisé* table is by Jules Leleu, 1938. The upholstered seating, a hybrid of mid-twentieth-century modernism and Louis XVI, is by Jed Johnson & Associates. Jean Pascaud's 1940 gilt-bronze sconces illuminate the room.

Overleaf: The hand-colored photograph by Luigi Ontani draws its imagery from ancient mythology, setting an unexpected tone in the formality of the dining room. Swedish painted and gilt chairs from the first quarter of the nineteenth century surround the custom-designed table.

Preceding page: A painting by Jonathan Lasker hangs above a Bugatti Chair on the window wall of the living room. The grouping of chairs demonstrates the blurring of the line between sculpture and decoration. The clients' own nineteenth-century Persian carpet, a family heirloom, unifies the space.

Right: The interior library was detailed and lit to become a perfect space for artworks on paper, susceptible to fading. The stone-top metal table is by the twentieth-century French master Gilbert Poillerat, and the ebonized and painted desk is late eighteenth-century Neapolitan.

EARLY YEARS

BY JAY JOHNSON

It is strange and interesting to revisit the past and see how a person's life unfolds. My brother Jed and I were born in Alexandria, a small farming town in northwestern Minnesota, in 1948. Although we were fraternal twins, our mother always dressed us in matching outfits. My hair was extremely curly, and she would pin curl Jed's so we would look identical. One thing she could not fix: my eyes were hazel, Jed's were brilliant blue. We were in the middle—two older brothers, Craig and Larry, and two younger sisters, Nancy and Susan. Like most twins, we were very close. Jed and I felt that closeness very often to the exclusion of others. One of my earliest memories is of jumping against the railing of my crib in order to move it across the room to Jed's. I crawled over the railings, and our mother found us together, sleeping.

During our first ten years, we lived in eight different houses, in town in the summertime, and by the lake in the winter. Rents were cheaper that way. Still, we grew up with the luxury of being able to play outdoors and could go pretty much anywhere without our parents worrying about us. Jed and I spent whole days walking in the fields and woods and by the many lakes. Our mother's only rule was that we could not go swimming without an adult. She said she had dreamt that one of us drowned.

Our favorite childhood pastime was building forts, mostly of branches, sticks, and leaves. During the winter we constructed intricate forts indoors with building blocks, which always transported us to other worlds. This was the beginning of Jed's lifelong passion for design.

When we were ten, the family left Minnesota and moved to Scottsdale, Arizona. Never having traveled beyond Fargo or Des Moines, Arizona was a cultural shock. We loved it: the high desert mountains, the heat, the cactus, the Indian reservation, and even the fear of scorpions and

Jed and Jay Johnson, Alexandria, Minnesota, 1949.

rattlesnakes. A great deal of development was going on in Scottsdale, and many tract homes were under construction nearby. Jed and I loved to play in the building sites, walking over the foundations and counting the rooms, discussing the floor plans and imagining the houses that would soon be built. We had never seen houses like these; they all seemed so big. We four boys all shared one bedroom growing up.

Our father's job in Scottsdale didn't work out, and in less than a year we moved to Sacramento, California, where he found work in construction. The last home that Jed and I actually lived in with our family was in a suburb called Fair Oaks, on the bluffs of the American River.

In Fair Oaks, we made interesting new friends. They were our introduction to art, reading, music, and travel. Two of our best friends were Joan Blunden and her brother Jeff. Joan was to become Joan Lunden of "Good Morning America" television fame. Their father was a physician and amateur pilot with his own small airport. Their mother was always organizing activities for us—ski trips to Lake Tahoe, lunch at the Palomino Club followed by a movie, or boating all day on Folsom Lake. Dr. Blunden gave us our first plane ride.

Joan had a friend named Barbara Klein (later Barbi Benton, girlfriend of Hugh Hefner.) Jed and Joan were junior high school sweethearts, as were Barbara and myself. Barbara lived in the biggest house that Jed and I had ever seen. It was the first home we had been inside that had a unique design, and we were impressed. From then on, we lost all interest in the tract homes in suburban Scottsdale and Sacramento.

While in high school Jed took a summer school class in architecture at American River Junior College. His professor was a devoted fan of Frank Lloyd Wright. Jed loved this class and was passionate about the subject. The professor was building a house for himself, made entirely of glass, stone, and wood. Jed and I visited the construction site with obsessive regularity. It was the first time he saw the degree of planning that building involved. He would have loved to continue his study of architecture, but he wasn't confident of his math skills and finances were not readily available for school.

When our parents' marriage ended, our father returned to Minnesota and our mother became the sole provider for the family. Jed and I decided to finish high school in the middle of our senior year and start college a semester early. We were able to get student loans and work on campus. The first semester was difficult, and by the end of the second we were ready for a break. We decided to take a semester off and drive cross-country to Montreal. We bought a used car for two hundred dollars—from money I had left over from my student loan and summer job—and left Sacramento right after Christmas, soon after our nineteenth birthday. Before we left Jed met two young soldiers at a rock concert in San Francisco and took LSD with them. One of the soldiers decided that he was going to desert rather than go to Vietnam. He was stationed at the army base in Sacramento, so we picked him up on our way out of town. Our first stop was San Francisco, where we went to the Fillmore and the Avalon Ballroom, saw Jimi Hendrix in concert, took drugs, and stayed in crash pads.

We drove to Los Angeles to tell our soldier friend's parents of his plans. On the way out of LA our car broke down, and we had to abandon it beside the Santa Monica Freeway. The next morning we started hitchhiking. Our first ride took us all the way to Albuquerque, New Mexico.

Jay and Jed Johnson with their mother, Vivian, California, 1961.

The sun was setting, and we were nervous about being in the middle of the desert with very little money. Fortunately, a car stopped just as we were about to despair. A couple with a baby needed to get to Chicago quickly, so we shared the driving and the cost of gas.

Our father happened to be visiting relatives in Chicago. It was the first time we had seen him since the divorce. He was not thrilled with our plans. In fact, he thought what we were doing was totally mad, but we had our minds made up; and besides, we weren't about to desert our deserter. It was so cold that we decided to continue to Montreal by train. We purchased tickets and left the next morning. Immigration authorities boarded the train somewhere near Buffalo. They assumed we were draft dodgers because we were teenagers with very little money and one-way tickets. Labeled "vagrants," we were forced to leave the train. We walked to the Greyhound bus station with our suitcases in hand, in our inadequate wardrobes, freezing, colder than I can ever remember, and purchased tickets to New York City.

We had heard that New York's East Village was the East Coast version of San Francisco's Haight-Ashbury. Asking for directions, we were told to take the subway to Astor Place and "you'll be there." When we emerged from the subway, still carrying our suitcases, someone directed us to St. Mark's Place and Second Avenue. St. Mark's was a carnival of head shops and vintage-clothing stores. At a hippie hangout on Seventh Street we met people who showed us to a crash pad on Rivington Street, where we spent our first night in the city. It was dirty, cold, and rat-infested; yet it was thrilling to be in New York on our own. The next day we began our search for a better place to stay. Our deserter friend hooked up with a girl who offered him refuge. They shacked up together until he was caught by the military police and sent to Fort Dix. Jed and I met a young couple over breakfast who took pity on us and generously offered us shelter. The next day we met a young man who said he would help us find an apartment. He took us around to look at different tenement buildings, getting more agitated as the day progressed. He turned out to be a heroin addict in need of a fix. We gave him twenty dollars, which he gratefully accepted. He had shown us an apartment that we thought we could afford on Tenth Street between Avenues A and B. We spoke to the super and rented the place for sixty-five dollars a month, no security deposit. It was a one-bedroom on the fourth floor of a walk-up tenement with the toilet in the hall and a bathtub in the kitchen. There were a few broken windows, which the super said he would fix and never did, but it had heat, hot water, and electricity. This was our first apartment, and we were very excited. The next morning we were mugged, and our jackets were stolen—there went our passports and all our money. We decided the only thing we could do was to wire our mother asking for help, a loan until we could find jobs; it was humbling but necessary. The Western Union agent sent the telegram, saying we could pay him when our money arrived. Mother came through. It was the best gift ever.

The agent said he needed people to deliver telegrams. The jobs paid $1.65 an hour plus tips, and we immediately said yes. On his third day Jed delivered a telegram to Paul Morrissey, the film director at Andy Warhol's new Factory on Union Square West. Paul asked Jed if he would like a job stripping windows, painting, and cleaning. Jed instantly agreed, seeing it as an opportunity to get inside from the cold, not even knowing who Andy Warhol was. When he told me about the job at the Factory, I informed him that Andy was a famous artist and underground filmmaker and rumored to be a homosexual. I said he was somehow involved with the rock group The Velvet

The Johnson twins on the beach in Montauk, Long Island, 1971.

Underground. Jed knew of them, of course—we were big fans and had played their album often. Jed soon realized that Andy was a truly great artist and that working at the Factory was a privilege.

The people who surrounded Andy where young, bright, talented, outrageous, often drugged, often beautiful, and incredibly interesting. Jed's real education began in this unique environment. He progressed from doing maintenance to assisting Paul on films to actually editing movies.

As a benefit of his newfound employment, Jed was allowed to sign for food at Max's Kansas City—an artists' hangout very popular at the time—using credit that Andy had obtained in exchange for one of his paintings. We would join Factory photographer Billy Name most nights for dinner at Max's, and he would always make us laugh. (Billy was the first "out" homosexual whom we met, and it was our association with him that helped Jed and me to come to terms with our own sexuality.) Andy's credit was used by many people who might not have eaten had he not been so generous.

Andy pretended not to believe that Jed and I were twins. He told everyone that we were only posing as twins and that we were really lovers because we were always whispering to each other and giggling. One evening Andy invited Jed and me out to see an underground play featuring one of his "superstars," Candy Darling. Neither Jed nor I knew that she was a transvestite, and Andy didn't let on. We did not realize until the end of the play when she appeared, nude, tied to a cross. We were shocked; she was so beautiful onstage as a woman. Afterward Andy took us to dinner at Max's, and Candy joined us. When the waitress asked us if we wanted a cocktail, Candy, realizing that at age nineteen I had no idea what to ask for, leaned over and said, "Darling, order a Black Russian, it's very good for growing men."

Andy dropped us off that evening, and when he saw our building he expressed concern that we were living in a bad neighborhood. Offering his help, he told Jed to find a better apartment. We found one on Seventeenth Street and Irving Place, another walk-up, this time six floors up, also with the bathtub in the kitchen and the toilet in the hall. There was key money to be paid, three hundred and fifty dollars, which Andy loaned Jed. We were now very close to the Factory and around the corner from Max's. Fred Hughes lived nearby at Sixteenth Street and Irving. Fred was Andy's business manager and a big part of the Factory scene. It was in his apartment that much of *Flesh*, the first movie on which Jed worked, was filmed. Fred had a great sense of style, and his small one-bedroom was beautifully decorated. Fred never took himself seriously and wanted everyone to have a good time. He always served his many guests champagne and caviar. His whimsical yet discerning way of creating an environment was part of his personality. It was from Fred that Jed got the first glimpses of what was meant by decorating.

It was not too long after Jed and I moved to Seventeenth Street that Valerie Solanas shot Andy. I was at home when a radio news brief interrupted, "Andy Warhol and possibly two others were shot by a deranged woman." I called the Factory. No answer. I ran to Union Square beside myself with fear. I begged a policeman to let me up to check on my twin brother. Fred was there. He and Jed had hidden from Valerie in the editing room, and then Jed had traveled to the hospital in the ambulance with Andy. I walked to Columbus Hospital praying all the way that Andy would survive. Jed was in the lobby crying. Andy had been shot numerous times, but, miraculously, he survived. During the following weeks it became Jed's ritual to visit Andy at the hospital a couple of times every day. He would also check on his mother, Julia Warhola, who lived with Andy. At the

Studio portrait of Jay and Jed Johnson, 1970. "God, they're both such beauties. Don't you wish you could look like that, Bob?" (Bob Colacello, quoting Andy Warhol)

Photograph: Jack Mitchell

hospital Jed would recount all the Factory gossip. During Andy's rehabilitation a deep relationship between them developed. When he left the hospital he asked Jed to come stay at his house at Eighty-ninth Street and Lexington to help care for him. Jed lived with Andy for the next twelve years.

The house on Lexington Avenue was like a warehouse. It was packed with objects from Andy's daily shopping trips. Nothing was organized; everything was piled wherever it would fit when Andy came home and set it down. Jed spent months trying to give order to the place, sending most of the stuff to the Factory to be stored. He decorated the house with the objects that he unearthed. Slowly, the place took shape and became livable, and rooms became recognizable as such. Andy's mother lived on the garden level with two cats. She was beginning to become senile, and it was increasingly difficult to care for her. Like Andy, she was a devout Roman Catholic. The house was located next door to a fertility clinic, and Mrs. Warhola was convinced that they were performing abortions. She said she could smell dead babies through the walls. One time Jed and Andy came home from the Factory and found her entertaining people she had met in the street. Andy loved his mother, and it was difficult for him to have her return home to Pittsburgh, where he thought she could be better cared for by other family members. It was a decision that pained him deeply.

Andy thought that it was a good time for them to move to a new house, and he asked Jed to find something special. The house he found was a beautiful Georgian-style townhouse on Sixty-sixth Street between Park and Madison Avenues. It was at the Sixty-sixth Street house that Jed honed his skills as a decorator. He had traveled extensively with Andy and seen great houses, which proved to be an invaluable learning experience for him. The project was a work of love that occupied much of his time for the next three years.

The interior painting was a major endeavor. Jed found Leo Sans, a traditional, old world–style painter from Connecticut. He asked Mr. Sans to paint the entrance foyer in six different shades of white. I thought he was crazy, but the result was amazing. I realized then that Jed had learned what made a great house great.

The curtain maker came from the Metropolitan Museum of Art and did freelance work for select clients. His craftsmanship was masterful; every fold was perfect with many hours of hand stitching. Jed found the most amazing nineteenth-century French wallpaper that was installed in Andy's bedroom as an element in the wainscoting, and he researched and designed intricate stenciling for the rest of the bedroom walls. He ordered special silk damask woven from the archives of Tassinari et Chatel, an ancient fabric house in France, for a pair of chairs in the Federalist-style sitting room. He waited six months for the fabric to be hand loomed. Jed sent my partner Tom Cashin and me to Paris especially to collect the bolt of silk. We were glad to be of service and had a great time in Paris . . . until we realized that we had left the roll of damask in the back window ledge of a taxi. I was afraid Jed would never speak to us again. The fabric had to be reordered, and, typical of Jed, the affair was never again mentioned.

Jed was decorating their townhouse when Andy asked him to direct the movie *Andy Warhol's Bad*, to be produced by Peter and Sandra Brant. The Brants were collectors of Andy's art and were backers of *Interview* magazine. Pat Hackett and George Abagnalo wrote the screenplay. (Pat was Jed's best friend at the Factory, and they saw each other or talked almost every day.) *Bad* was supposed to be Andy's entrance into legitimate cinema, and he put a lot of pressure on Jed to get it right, which

Photo booth photograph of Jay, Susan, and Jed Johnson at Studio 54, 1978.

caused a great deal of strain on their relationship. Vincent Canby of The *New York Times* gave *Bad* a favorable review, calling it a film "more aware of what it's up to than any Andy Warhol film I've seen to date." He compared its deadpan style to the late English playwright Joe Orton's works *Entertaining Mr. Sloane* and *Loot*. Though *Bad* has become a cult classic and one of the most acclaimed Warhol films, the movie was not a financial success. Jed was discouraged by the whole experience and never again worked in film, spending less time at the Factory and more decorating the house.

When the townhouse was completed, everyone was curious to see it and dying for an invitation, but Andy was very private and did not like to have people over. Many of his friends never got past the front steps. Pierre Bergé, of Yves St. Laurent, was one of the few exceptions. After seeing Andy's interiors and having recently purchased an apartment at the Pierre Hotel, he asked Jed to be in charge of his decoration. It was Jed's first professional commission. He was thrilled and overwhelmed. To help him with the project, he asked friend and American furniture expert Judith Hollander to collaborate. I was hired as secretary, bookkeeper, and decorating assistant, which meant that I got to return fabric samples to the D & D Building, but I was also able to learn the design business. Pierre allowed Jed and Judith to put together a remarkable collection of nineteenth-century American furniture, paintings, and objects. Jed's painstakingly researched stencil designs for the walls and ceilings created a sensation. The fact that he had no professional training saved him from the stylistic prejudices of the time. He was free to make beautiful rooms unselfconsciously. In May 1979 the Bergé apartment was published in *Vogue*, introducing Jed's talent to the public, and he quickly rose to prominence in the international design world. Realizing that he needed help with interior architecture on various projects, he often gave commissions to Alan Wanzenberg, an I. M. Pei architect who worked freelance on the side. Their collaboration developed into a personal relationship, and in December 1980 Jed moved out of the townhouse and into an apartment he had bought on West Sixty-seventh Street. Alan moved in with him. The most difficult part of this transition for Jed was the shared custody of Archie and Amos, the two beloved dachshunds he and Andy had raised from puppies.

Alan soon left I. M. Pei and formed a business with Jed. Later, for professional reasons, they formed two separate companies and continued to collaborate on most projects until Jed's death in 1996. After the tragedy of Jed's death, I made the decision that his design firm should not close but should remain in existence as part of his legacy. Jed Johnson Associates continues today with most of the same designers who worked personally with him, including Arthur Dunnam, Christine Cain, Buzz Kelly, and Andy Clark.

Jed's life evolved in a fascinating way. He achieved success and acclaim as an interior designer, but what people who knew him remember most was his remarkable character. He was deeply principled. His sense of integrity was the cornerstone of his career. He never compromised about giving the most of himself to a friend or a project, always striving for the highest quality. What I will remember most was the quality of his love. When Jed died, the deep emotional connection that we had as twins was forever gone. Losing that special intimacy, which I often took for granted, makes me realize what a precious gift I was given. Now, as president of Jed Johnson Associates, I hope to continue the work Jed began and ensure its lasting presence. A recently developed new company, Jed Johnson Home, offers textiles, furniture, and home accessories in a way that honors Jed, with designs that I know would make him proud.

Andy Warhol, Jed, and Jay Johnson at the Factory, 1969. "Getting close to genius is dangerous—and no one got closer to Andy Warhol than Jed Johnson." (Bob Colacello)

Photograph: Cecil Beaton, courtesy of Cecil Beaton Studio Archive, Sotheby's

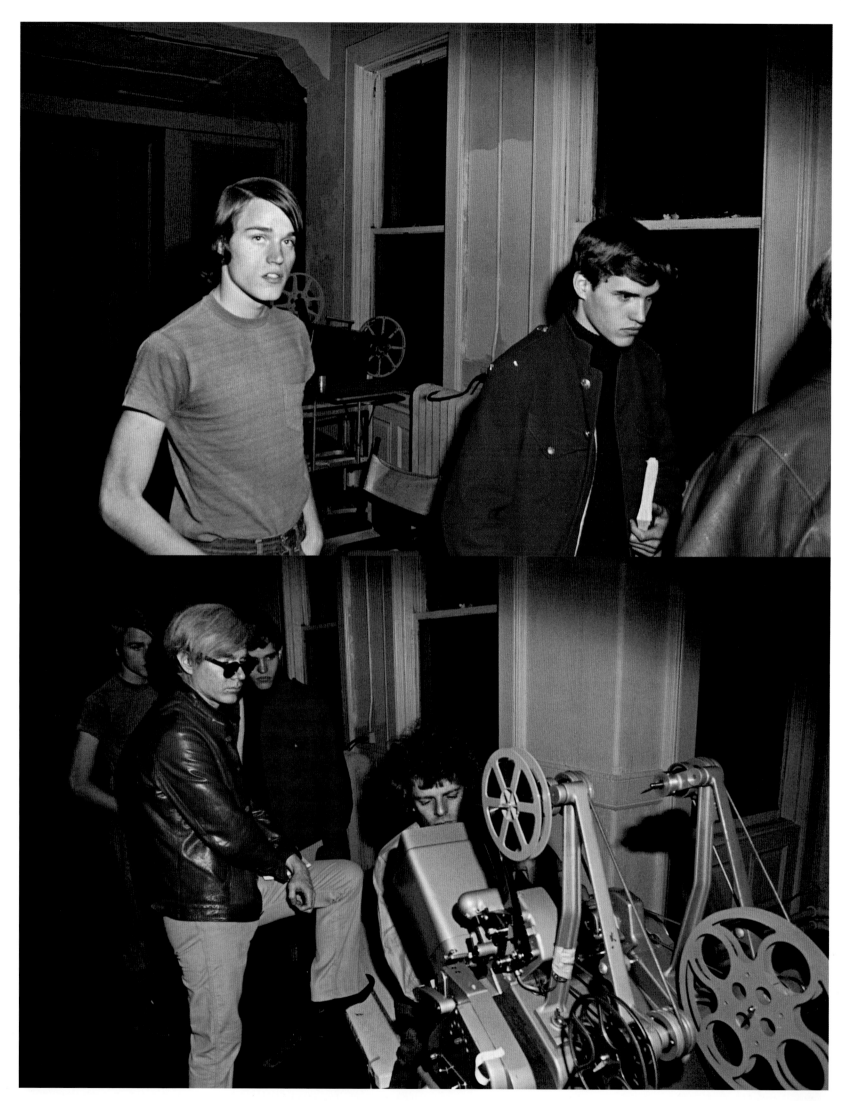

JED JOHNSON REMEMBERED

BY BOB COLACELLO

"God, they're both such beauties. Don't you wish you could look like that, Bob?"
—Andy Warhol, talking about Jed and Jay Johnson, circa 1972

Jed Johnson and I worked together for a decade, side by side on the assembly line at Andy Warhol's Factory. When I started in 1970, as a twenty-five-dollar-per-review film critic for *Interview*, the magazine Warhol had launched the previous year, Jed was editing *Andy Warhol's Women in Revolt*, a comedy starring the transvestites Candy Darling, Holly Woodlawn, and Jackie Curtis as members of a feminist group called Politically Involved Girls. I remember Jed giggling every time Paul Morrissey, who directed the film, pointed out to visitors that the acronym for Politically Involved Girls was PIGS and that the fictional movement's leaders were based on Gloria Steinem, Betty Friedan, and Germaine Greer. I also remember Jed sitting in a tiny editing room, patiently cutting and re-cutting the same scene over and over again while an indecisive Paul stood over his shoulder nudging him to try it yet another way.

It was Paul who had hired Jed in the first place, when he delivered a telegram to the Factory one day in the winter of 1968. Jed and his twin brother, Jay, had moved to New York only two weeks earlier from Fair Oaks, California, a suburb of Sacramento; they had both dropped out of college—Jed from American River College, Jay from Sacramento State—and were working for Western Union to pay the rent. "What's a good-looking kid like you doing delivering telegrams?" asked Paul. "We'll pay you the same amount of money to sweep the floors, and teach you about the art and movie businesses." Jed immediately accepted, and soon Jay started getting modeling jobs through his brother's new connections.

Vertical diptych of Jed and Jay Johnson, Andy Warhol, and Paul Morrissey at the Factory, 1968. Jed "progressed from doing maintenance to assisting Paul on the films to actually editing movies." (Jay Johnson)

Photograph: Billy Name

In June of that year, Andy was shot and nearly killed by Valerie Solanas, a deranged Factory hanger-on who told the press that he "controlled her life." Jed rode in the ambulance with Andy, who would require a five-hour operation by a team of five surgeons because his would-be assassin's three bullets, fired at close range, had pierced every vital organ except his heart. After Andy was released from the hospital, Jed moved into his house on Lexington Avenue, near Eighty-ninth Street, to help his mother, Julia, a Czechoslovak immigrant who barely spoke English, care for him. During the long months of Andy's recuperation, he and Jed fell in love.

Jed would become Andy's interior decorator-in-residence at the East Sixty-sixth Street townhouse he bought in 1975, and eventually the director of *Andy Warhol's Bad*, the first Factory film not directed by Paul Morrissey. His best friend at the factory, Pat Hackett, wrote the script for *Bad*, which, among other things, was supposed to be a comeback vehicle for Carroll Baker, but it instead turned out to be a swan song for pretty much everyone involved. Fours years after it was released, Jed and Andy separated, and Jed left the home he had so beautifully arranged to start a new life and business with the architect Alan Wanzenberg on the other side of Central Park.

In 1971, I moved up to managing editor and art director of the fledgling *Interview*—print run five thousand—at a salary of fifty dollars a week. For a middle-class twenty-two-year-old from Long Island, the Factory was exciting but frightening: the Warhol gang had a reputation for both wildness and exclusivity. Its habitués seemed to come from either the tough streets of the East Village or the plush co-ops of Fifth and Park Avenues, and while Andy and Paul gave me their full support, I spent many months enduring Joe Dallesandro's scowls and Brigid Berlin's sneers. Andy's business manager, Fred Hughes, with his hand-tailored suits and high-society flourishes, blew hot and cold, embracing me after a few glasses of champagne at some fancy party that Andy had dragged me to, whispering behind my back about how "bourgeois" I was the next day at work. Then there were the times when Solanas, who served a mere three years in a mental institution because a terrified Andy had refused to press charges, called and growled to whomever answered the telephone, "Is Warhol there?" (Andy would lock himself in the editing room with Jed, while Joe stood guard at the bulletproof steel door that separated the Factory's front room from the vestibule and elevator, and Vincent Fremont, Warhol's bookkeeper-cum–video director, went downstairs to make sure that the coast was clear for "the boss" to escape uptown in a taxi.)

It would be an exaggeration to say that Jed became my protector—he had his hands full pleasing Paul and taking care of Andy—but at least he was *nice*. He smiled and asked me how I was doing. He invited me to have lunch with him and Pat at Brownie's, the health-food restaurant just off Union Square where they went every day—but only occasionally, because Pat was very possessive of Jed and probably a little in love with him. But then, I think nearly everyone at the Factory was a little in love with Jed, including my straight assistant editor, Glenn O'Brien, and his first wife, Judy (aka Jude Jade). There was something so appealing about Jed's shyness and calm. He spoke so softly you had to lean in close to hear what he was saying; he often said nothing at all while the rest of us babbled on, competing to be the wittiest for Andy and his tape recorder. Jed didn't try to be smart or funny or anything at all; he was incapable of showing off; he just was what he was: a slim, silent beauty in perfectly pressed jeans and neatly checked shirts, as handsome and intriguing as the young Gary Cooper, a sweet, innocent fawn among the tigresses and hyenas.

Jed Johnson with Jane Forth at the opening of the Whitney Museum of American Art exhibition of Andy Warhol works, 1971. Forth would later appear in Johnson's movie *Andy Warhol's Bad*.

Perhaps that was why Andy, lion king of this hothouse jungle, liked having Jed live with him: he was so easy to be with, so quiet and serene. Or so it appeared. I remember Jed in tears once, in Rome, where he was editing *Andy Warhol's Frankenstein* and *Andy Warhol's Dracula*, after a fight with Jay, who had managed to topple a bathroom sink off its base while putting on his makeup for a party we were giving at our rented villa, causing a flood and almost ruining the night. Jed and I had a heart-to-heart talk after the guests left and his brother fled in anger, and I saw then that staying calm wasn't as easy as he made it seem.

After a couple of years at the Factory I developed a severe case of anemia and decided to run off to Puerto Vallarta for the summer, turning over the editorship of *Interview* to Glenn O'Brien. I was there for about a month when Andy called and begged me to come back, saying that Glenn and Paul were at each other's throats—"They're both too Irish to get along" was the way he put it. I resisted, saying that I was just starting to feel better and wasn't sure if I wanted to continue working for him in any case. "Oh, Jed wants to talk to you," Andy said. I can still hear that faraway voice, whispery but determined; "Oh, hi, Bob. When are you coming home? Everyone misses you, especially me."

And so I returned and had many more good times and not-so-good times with Jed and Andy and Fred and Paul and Pat and Brigid and Vincent and Ronnie Cutrone and all the other "kids," as Warhol called his Factory workers, who came and went during the long stretch that followed.

One of the unhappiest days was December 24, 1980, the day Jed decided to tell Andy he was leaving him. Marina Schiano—the fiery Neapolitan who ran Yves St. Laurent's business in America and was so much a part of the Warhol family that she was even briefly married to Fred Hughes—called me with the shocking news. "How can he do it on Christmas Eve?" she screeched. "I understand why he is doing it, but you cannot—you cannot—leave poor Andy, monster that he is, on Christmas Eve!" Marina had been instrumental in getting Jed his first decorating job—Pierre Bergé's apartment at the Pierre Hotel—several years earlier, and loved him dearly, but she could not understand why he wouldn't wait until after the holidays had passed to move out of Andy's house. By then, I could.

Getting close to a genius is dangerous—and no one got closer to Andy Warhol than Jed Johnson. Yet Andy didn't tell him that his mother had died; he found out accidentally, two or three years later from one of Andy's brothers. Geniuses do things like that, especially to those they love the most, or should I say, to those who love them the most. From a distance they dazzle, up close they often destroy those who help them create. I always thought Jed stayed with Andy as long as he did because he felt sorry for him—he seemed so helpless and unhappy underneath the disco wig. I know that was a big part of why I stayed. A year after Jed left the Factory, however, I finally found the guts to walk away too. His example had inspired me, and I told him that when he called a few days later. Typically, he didn't lambaste Andy or complain about the years he had spent with him, but simply said, "I'm so happy for you, Bob. And I know how you feel."

Andy never really recovered from the break-up with Jed. He pretended he didn't mind, telling anyone who asked, "Oh, it's just one less problem." But during the following year he signed up with the Zoli modeling agency, starved himself down to 120 pounds, and hounded *Interview*'s advertisers and photographers to use him in their shoots and fashion shows. It was as if he wanted

Johnson on the set of *Bad* with Perry King and Susan Tyrrell, 1976. *Bad* "was not a financial success. Jed was discouraged by the whole experience and never again worked in film. *Bad* has since become a cult classic and is one of Andy's most acclaimed movies." (Jay Johnson)

Photograph: Pat Hackett

to convince the world that he, too, could be a beauty—his favorite noun—that he didn't need or care about the beauty who had fled. In February 1987, Andy died of heart failure after gallbladder surgery at age fifty-eight. He and Jed were on speaking terms by then—Jed would pick up their pet dachshunds, Archie and Amos, every weekend—and Jed was seated up front at the big funeral in St. Patrick's Cathedral, along with Fred Hughes, Vincent Fremont, Pat Hackett, and Brigid Berlin, all of whom had stuck with Andy until the unexpected end.

Jed's end came prematurely, too. He was flying to Paris to shop for one of the many rich and famous clients—the Brants, the Lauders, Mick Jagger—he and Alan had acquired over the years; because he was a good customer, TWA called and offered him an upgrade from business to first class if he wanted to fly out one night earlier. I was at my house at Amagansett on the night of July 17, 1996, when the news came on the television that Flight 800 had exploded over the Atlantic Ocean off Long Island a few minutes after taking off from John F. Kennedy Airport. From the footage played over and over on every network, it appeared that some sort of flaring object had hit the 747 and broken it in two; people who lived in Westhampton, near where the pieces of the plane fell into the ocean, swore they had seen a missile heading toward the plane. There was immediate speculation about terrorists armed with a stinger; later, when it was learned that the U.S. Navy carried out exercises at a nearby naval base, suspicion grew that our own military had accidentally shot down the airliner. After years of investigation, a government panel attributed the crash to technical problems, but a sense of mystery remains.

On that horrible night, however, the cause seemed immaterial. I heard the news first from Marina Schiano: Jed was on that plane. "How unfair God is," she railed. "Why does he take the best first—the sweetest! the gentlest! the nicest!—and leave the worst for last? He was like a lamb, Jed was. It's not right, it's not just! Oh how, oh why, can Jed be gone like this, so young, so handsome, so full of life?"

I came into the city the following day, and went with Marina and Doris Ammann to the apartment on West Sixty-seventh Street that Jed shared with Alan Wanzenberg. I remember Jay crying softly to Doris, who had lost her brother, Thomas, three years before. I remember Jay's longtime boyfriend, Tom Cashin, who always had the biggest, brightest smile, struck dumb with shock and grief. I remember Fran Lebowitz, out of quips for once in her life, pacing the floor and chain-smoking. I remember Pat Hackett on the phone for hours with the FAA and TWA, trying to recover Jed's body.

For the rest of that summer, remnants of Flight 800—bits of metal, life preservers, paper cups marked TWA—washed ashore on the beaches of the Hamptons, including the one down the road from my house, sending a shiver down the spine of those who stumbled upon these reminders of the fragility of our high-tech existence and the temporary nature of life. As for Jed's corpse, it was one of the few found whole, barely bruised, a beauty to the end.

Alan Wanzenberg and Jed Johnson, partners in life and frequent collaborators in architecture and design, 1995.
Photograph: John Hall

JED JOHNSON

BY SANDRA J. BRANT

Although by now it's a famous bit of Factory lore that Jed Johnson first appeared in Andy Warhol's life as a Western Union boy delivering a telegram, nobody seems to remember what the urgent message inside the envelope actually said. Clearly, Jed, who was a quiet one, stole the sender's thunder. But I always like to imagine that on that piece of paper was written: "Take note of the newcomer in front of your eyes, and give him a job STOP One day he will be a legend STOP He will be known as the man who put the *interior* back into interior design STOP."

To me the interior life of a space is the key to the difference between a room overseen by Jed and the work of so many other designers. Jed's rooms never seem weighed down by a sense of importance or by the smell of money, both of which can make a place feel cold and dead. A room by Jed feels lived in, the objects loved for what they are, not because they are trophies. Together everything—the furniture, the paintings, the fabrics, the decorative objects—seems to belong in the space, as if it has all finally come home and can at last breathe a sigh of relief. Such a sensation is not possible without an acute sensitivity to architecture and place, which Jed had in spades.

I am often asked, "Why did you choose Jed as your interior designer when you did? You could have picked anyone, so why go with such an unknown, inexperienced person?" The truth is that we fell into a relationship. By about 1974, when we started to formally work together, we'd already done so much else together, it was a natural progression of our friendship—and our belief in Jed's respect for architecture, his love of craft, and his interest in the life of objects, all of which he never betrayed. Our relationship began when my husband at the time, Peter Brant, and I were collecting Pop Art. We became close to Andy and Jed, who had started living together soon after they met—in fact, during the critical juncture in Andy's life, when he was shot. The four of us

Jed and Andy outside the townhouse at 57 East Sixty-sixth Street, 1977. "Everyone was curious to see it and dying for an invitation, but Andy was very private and did not like to have people over. Many of his friends never got past the front steps." (Jay Johnson)

spent so much time around each other that we knew each other through and through. We tossed our hats in together on various projects, including *Interview* magazine. And, of course, the early 1970s were the Golden Age for the unforgettable and extremely influential movies that came out of the Factory, films that Jed contributed to in no small way. We had witnessed his patience and tenacity as an editor on *Trash* and on *Frankenstein*, and we had seen him quietly—but effectively, make no mistake about that—exert his authority as the director of *Bad*.

During all that, it was obvious why Jed was a constant light in Andy's orbit of extra-terrestrials, shooting stars, fireballs, inspired individuals, and earthly cohorts. Jed "got it"—all of it. He was talented in his own right, yet he was also great at recognizing and bringing out the brilliance of others, qualities that would eventually soar in his work as an interior designer. He would seek out incredible craftsmen, and then pull the best out of them. Jed's ability to recognize something inspired was there right from the start.

I can't really untangle when it was that he became "Jed the interior designer." But, I guess, it's possible to pinpoint the moment when he went, as they say, "professional." A few things happened simultaneously. Andy's house at 57 East Sixty-sixth Street was done by Jed; and our Colorado house, designed by Robert Venturi, had an interior by Jed, who also co-owned it with us.

But really, Jed's love for his subject became manifest earlier in the '70s, in the treasure hunts that we would all go on together for what had become our mutual obsession: Art Deco. Frank, Ruhlmann, and Legrain weren't the buzz names then that they have become. In fact, the entire field was tiny and unmined, and there was a delicious sense of secrecy and discovery to collecting it. Karl Lagerfeld, Yves Saint Laurent, Pierre Bergé, Ileana Sonnabend, and Henry Geldzahler were practically the only other obsessed fans of the stuff. Somewhere in all of this—in the exhilaration that comes with learning, discovering, and finding not just material things but extraordinary examples of the human need to imbue places and objects with beauty and soul—Jed and I bonded.

Over the years that bond would ultimately take us on dozens of adventures—to learn, to see, to find—to factories, museums, antiques shops, historic houses, and all sorts of memorable places. Whether we were on those excursions as pals casually doing things together, which is how it all began, or as client and decorator, which is the relationship that eventually transpired, we always had such fun. Whether we were on a research trip to Vita Sackville-West's beloved Sissinghurst, or going to a factory in England to persuade the owners to pull out the old blocks that William Morris had used and re-create wallpaper that hadn't been made for decades, one could tell that Jed loved the histories and stories that came with these excursions.

There's an indelible image I have of Jed. He's doing headstands and backflips on our lawn, which he used to do to entertain the kids. Well, he brought that same joy, and willingness to do what it took—because he cared so much—to his work. No doubt the work got "better" as Jed went along, because as the years added up Jed, who had begun with no formal education in architecture and design, had learned so much, visited so many places, looked at so many books. But here's the fact: His work was kind of perfect from the beginning. Like J. H. Lartigue, he had the uncanny instinct of a visionary, enthusiastic amateur. Whether one describes Jed's talent as an eye, a calling, or a natural ability, it doesn't matter. What counts is that when one walks into a room created by Jed Johnson, one always feels at home.

A four-portrait painting of Jed Johnson by Andy Warhol, 1973.

ACKNOWLEDGMENTS

Special appreciation is extended to the talented writers and photographers whose contributions made this book a reality, and to art director Takaaki Matsumoto. We also wish to gratefully acknowledge the assistance of numerous others who were helpful in the production of *Jed Johnson: Opulent Restraint*. They include Hisami Aoki, Alexander Antonelli, Tristan Béchard, Sam Bolton, Russell Bowden, Greg Burchard, Vance Burke, Christine Cain, Andy Clark, John Clausen, Maureen Cogan, Ann Black Cone, Christine Cordazzo, Douglas Curran, Tony Decal, Beth Rudin de Woody, Barbaralee Diamonstein-Spielvogel, Peter Eyre, Gretchen Fenston, Vincent Fremont, Katryna Glettler, Allan Greenberg, Pat Hackett, Jonathan Hogg, Deborah Hughes, Tim Hunt, Vivian Johnson Christophier, Erin Kane, Paul Kasmin, Buzz Kelly, Robert Kirkland, Kevin Kushel, Jessalyn Kwak, Peter Lang, Joan Lunden, David Masello, Marcy Masterson, David Meitus, Charles Miers, Farimah Milani, Leigh Montville, Senga Mortimer, David Morton, Ellen Nidy, Mona Perlhagen, Anet Sirna-Bruder, Pam Sommers, Michael Stier, Ippolita Passigli, Connie Uzzo, Barbara Von Schreiber, John W. Smith, Etheleen Staley, Angela Westwater, Amy Wilkins, Stephanie Winston Wolkoff, and Takouhy Wise.

Jed emerging from the water, 1974.